dBASE IV® SmartStart

Jean S. Insinga
Middlesex Community-Technical College

Marianne B. Fox

Lawrence C. Metzelaar

College

dBASE IV SmartStart

Copyright © 1993 by Que® Corporation.

Library of Congress Catalog No.: 93-83866

ISBN: 1-56529-251-0

96 95 94 93   4 3 2

Interpretation of the printing code: the rightmost double-digit number is the year of the book's printing; the rightmost single-digit number, the number of the book's printing. For example, a printing code of 93-1 shows that the first printing of the book occurred in 1993.

Screens reproduced in this book were created using Collage Plus from Inner Media, Inc., Hollis, NH.

dBASE IV SmartStart is based on Release 1.1 of dBASE IV.

Publisher: David P. Ewing

Associate Publisher: Rick Ranucci

Product Development Manager: Thomas A. Bennett

Operations Manager: Sheila Cunningham

Book Designer: Scott Cook

Production Team: Jeff Baker, Danielle Bird, Julie Brown, Brad Chinn, Brook Farling, Heather Kaufman, Bob LaRoche, Caroline Roop, Linda Seifert, Amy Steed

Indexers: Michael Hughes, Joy Dean Lee

About the Authors

Jean S. Insinga is Professor of Information Systems and Accounting at Middlesex Community-Technical College in Middletown, Connecticut. She has an extensive background in the computer programming and application software fields. She is also the author of *WordPerfect 5.1 SmartStart*, published by Que Corporation, and *The Prentice Hall Computerized Accounting Practice Sets*. Jean has earned B.S. and M.S. degrees from Central Connecticut State University. She also holds a C.A.I.S. (Computer Applications Information Systems) certificate from the University of New Haven.

Marianne B. Fox holds a fulltime faculty position with Butler University, Indianapolis, Indiana, where she teaches a variety of accounting and computer-related courses. She is coauthor of 12 books for Que Corporation, including *dBASE IV QuickStart*, *dBASE IV 1.1 QuickStart*, *Introduction to Business Software*, and *WordPerfect 5.1 Workbook and Disk*.

Lawrence C. Metzelaar holds associate faculty positions at Purdue University, West Lafayette, Indiana, and Vincennes University, Vincennes, Indiana, where he teaches microcomputer classes. He also teaches microcomputer continuing education seminars at Indiana and Ohio State Universities. He is coauthor of 12 books for Que Corporation, including *dBASE IV QuickStart*, *dBASE IV 1.1 QuickStart*, *Introduction to Business Software*, and *WordPerfect 5.1 Workbook and Disk*.

Title Manager
Carol Crowell

Senior Editor
Jeannine Freudenberger

Production Editor
Barb Colter

Editors
Jo Anna Wittman Arnott
Fran Blauw
Kelly Currie

Editorial Assistant
Elizabeth D. Brown

Trademarks

Composed in *Garamond* and *MCPdigital* by Que Corporation

Give Your Computer Students
a SmartStart on the Latest
Computer Applications

Que's SmartStart series from Prentice Hall Computer Publishing combines the experience of the Number 1 computer book publisher in the industry with the pedagogy you've come to expect in a textbook.

SmartStarts cover just the basics in a format filled with plenty of step-by-step instructions and screen shots.

Each SmartStart chapter ends with a "Testing Your Knowledge" section that includes true/false, multiple choice, and fill-in-the-blank questions; two or three short projects, and two long projects. The long projects are continued throughout the book to help students build on skills learned in preceding chapters.

Each SmartStart comes with an instructor's manual featuring additional test questions, troubleshooting tips, and additional exercises. This manual will be available both on disk and bound.

Look for the following additional SmartStarts:

Word for Windows SmartStart	1-56529-204-9
Excel 4 for Windows SmartStart	1-56529-202-2
MS-DOS SmartStart	1-56529-249-9
WordPerfect 5.1 SmartStart	1-56529-246-4
Lotus 1-2-3 SmartStart (covers 2.4 and below)	1-56529-245-6
Windows 3.1 SmartStart	1-56529-203-0

For more information call:

1-800-428-5331

or contact your local Prentice Hall College Representative

Contents at a Glance

Table of Contents

Introduction

This book, *dBase IV SmartStart*, is designed for a hands-on computer course in database management, enabling you to structure your topics within the time frame of your curriculum. Whether you are a novice or a user of a previous version of dBASE, this Smartstart is one of the easiest and fastest ways to master the Control Center environment of dBASE IV.

The book takes you through dBASE IV with step-by-step exercises within the chapters, describing all the fundamentals you need to know about the software. Each chapter begins with an overview and objectives to be covered in each chapter. At the end of each chapter, you will be able to test your knowledge, completing questions and projects to reinforce the material covered in the chapter.

Who Should Use This Book

dBASE IV Smartstart is designed primarily for new users of dBASE IV, but you can benefit from it even if you already know something about database management programs. If you want to master the basics of dBASE IV quickly, this book is for you.

This book assumes that the dBASE IV software already is installed on your hard drive system.

How To Use This Book

Chapters 1 through 7 are organized so that you create; maintain (add, edit, and delete data); and use the database (index, search, and print). You should at least read Chapters 1 through 4 before attempting other chapters in the text.

Chapters 8 and 9 address custom-designing your own data entry screens and reports. Chapter 8 addresses in detail the procedures to attach fields to a work surface. If your time frame for the course is limited, you can work with Chapter 9, "Designing Custom Reports," before working with Chapter 8.

How This Book Is Organized

Chapter 1, "Getting Started," explains how to start and leave dBASE IV and teaches you the basics about the keyboard, the Control Center, menus and work surfaces, the Help feature, and basic print procedures.

Chapter 2, "Designing and Creating a Database," illustrates basic database design techniques and shows you how to create, edit, save, and print a database structure.

Chapter 3, "Editing Data," demonstrates three main topics: entering and editing records in Browse or Edit mode, executing Browse Fields options, and using Memo fields.

Chapter 4, "Organizing Data," explains indexing as opposed to sorting; teaches you to create, modify, and remove an index; and illustrates how to edit with an index in control.

Chapter 5, "Conducting Simple Searches from the Data Panel," explains positioning the record pointer, searching forward and backward for records that exactly match a specified condition, and searching an indexed database.

Chapter 6, "Creating Simple Queries," introduces creating queries to limit both the records and fields available for display. Illustrations are limited to display of records whose field contents exactly match one or more search conditions based on character, numeric, data, and logical data.

Chapter 7, "Creating Complex Queries," teaches you to create queries which select records based on a search condition other than an exact match. Illustrations include using relational operators, using summary operators, searching on partial contents of a field, searching for a phonetic approximation of actual data, establishing multiple search conditions, and sorting query results.

Chapter 8, "Designing Custom Screens," explains how to design, create, save, and use custom screens. Illustrations include using templates, picture functions, and Edit options to control data entry.

Chapter 9, "Designing Custom Reports," explains how to design, create, save and use custom reports. Topics include using Quick layout options and enhancing the appearance of printed output.

Where To Find More Help

After you learn the fundamentals presented in this book, you may want to learn more advanced applications of dBASE IV. Que Corporation has a full line of dBASE IV books you can use. Among these are *Using dBASE IV* and *dBASE IV PC Tutor*.

You can use dBASE IV's Help feature to answer some of your questions while you work with dBASE IV. Using Help is explained and illustrated in Chapter 1, "Getting Started."

Conventions Used in This Book

Certain conventions are used throughout the text and graphics of *dBASE IV SmartStart* to help you understand the book.

Within step-by-step instructions, references to keys are as they appear on the keyboard of the IBM Personal Computer and most IBM-compatibles. When two keys appear together, for example, ⟨⇧Shift⟩+⟨F2⟩, you press and hold down the first key as you also press the second key. Release both keys at the same time. Other key combinations, such as ⟨Ctrl⟩+⟨Esc⟩ or ⟨Alt⟩+⟨F⟩, are pressed in the same manner. In numbered steps, these keys appear in blue.

To select a menu option means to highlight the option and press ⟨↵Enter⟩. Information that you type, such as NAME, appears in blue and boldface in numbered steps or in boldface in regular text.

Getting Started

The dBASE IV program is a powerful database that enables you to organize your data into meaningful files that you can access quickly. Imagine a room filled with file cabinets. Now imagine having to access your data by searching through each folder in each cabinet. Suppose that each drawer of each file cabinet represents a file in dBASE IV. By using dBASE IV, you can create your files and then manipulate your abundant data into meaningful and timely reports for management decisions.

You will find it relatively easy to start dBASE IV, complete your activity, and exit the program if you take the time to acquire some general knowledge in advance. Don't be tempted to skip to the end of this section and start the dBASE IV program without first understanding these topics: the layout of the dBASE IV features and the keys used to access them, the meaning of screen displays, the operation of the Help feature, and the procedure used to produce a Quick report.

Objectives

1. To Start dBASE IV
2. To Understand Menus and Work Surfaces
3. To Use Keyboard Keys
4. To Use the Help Screens
5. To Use Basic Print Options
6. To Navigate the Control Center
7. To Exit dBASE IV

1

Key Terms Used in This Chapter	
Control Center	A dBASE IV screen display that provides access to a system of pull-down menus governing many dBASE features.
Control Center panels	Six menu options from which you can create and maintain files (Data, Forms, Reports, Labels) and run queries, searches, or applications.
Work surface	A complete screen display except for the menu bar at the top of the screen and the information area at the bottom of the screen (status bar, navigation line, and message line), a dynamically changing work area used to control dBASE IV.
Menu bar	A horizontal menu appearing on the top row of a work-surface screen.
Pull-down menu	A menu, accessed from the menu bar, in which the options are listed one after another in a single column.
Status bar	A dynamically changing bar, located below the work surface, that contains five sections of information about the status of dBASE IV.
Navigation line	A line below the status bar that displays the keys you use to move the cursor for that particular task or file.
Message line	A line at the bottom of the screen that provides instructions about the current operation.
Catalog	A group of related database file names. A catalog should not be confused with a directory. Catalogs do not contain the files themselves—only the file names.

An Overview of Databases and Database Programs

A database is defined as a group of related records and files. Databases have existed for many years in the business, medical, academic, and political environments. Companies and organizations have relied on complex manual methods to organize data so that it can be available for making timely and accurate reports and decisions. With the huge amounts of data that businesses amass, computerizing databases became inevitable.

A computerized database consists of a collection of records stored in a *file*. Each *record* contains the same *fact types* arranged in the same order. In a computerized database, these fact types are known as *fields*, and the facts contained in each field are referred to as *data*. Each field are given a *length* and a *type* (numeric, character, and so on). A computerized database program is a software application that enables you to create and maintain your own database.

Imagine a sales person with thousands customers in various states; these customers need to be serviced on certain days of the week in each given month. Providing such service may seem complicated, but a database program will provide accurate information at the correct time.

Before you can truly understand how databases work, look at a simple example. Examine the following records with selected fields:

Record 1: Shoreline Liquor	210 Hill Drive	CT 1
Record 2: The Yellow Front	Bank Street	CT 3
Record 3: Warehouse Beverage	Golden Road	MA 8
Record 4: Local Watering Hole	1234 Sipps Lane	CT 3

Each preceding record consists of a group of fields. Notice that each field for each record holds the same type of information: the customer name, address, state, and day of month to be serviced. This data is available in a manual system on a card holder, of course, but collecting the information is a cumbersome and time-consuming task. Using a database program, however, you set up fields, specify the type of field (numeric or character) and field size, and then enter the data from the individual records.

1

The database design then lists the specifications for each field, as follows:

Field 1: CustName	Type: Character	Width: 15
Field 2: Address	Type: Character	Width: 15
Field 3: State	Type: Character	Width: 2
Field 4: Day	Type: Numeric	Width: 2

You can change this design at any time; you can add, change, or delete fields. After you have created the database and added the records, the database looks like this:

CustName	Address	State	Day
Shoreline Liquor	210 Hill Drive	CT	1
The Yellow Front	Bank Street	CT	3
Warehouse Beverage	Golden Road	MA	8
Local Watering Hole	1234 Sipps Lane	CT	3

You can also print reports from the finished database.

As you work with dBASE IV, you will learn how to search a database and select only the records requested. Remember, for example, the sales person who has a thousand customers and needs a list of all customers to service on day 3. Using the commands in dBASE IV, the sales person can easily get a list of all customers to service on day 3. The user also can sort the records, that is, arrange them in a variety of different ways. These capabilities provide a company with speed and accuracy to increase productivity in the business environment.

Objective 1: To Start dBASE IV

If you turn on your computer and a menu of program names appears (such as a word processing program, a spreadsheet program, and dBASE IV), you need to choose only the number of the dBASE IV option in order to access the dBASE program.

If you see an operating system prompt (for example, C>) when you turn on your computer, however, you must set the current directory to the location of your dBASE program.

Exercise 1.1: Accessing dBASE

To access dBASE IV, follow these steps:

1. Select the dBASE IV option from your Custom menu, or type **dbase** and press ⏎Enter. The dBASE IV logo screen appears. A few seconds later, the copyright screen appears automatically (see figs. 1.1 and 1.2).

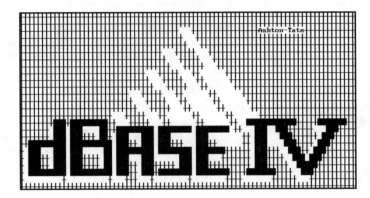

Fig.1.1
The dBASE IV
logo screen.

2. Follow the screen instructions and then press ⏎Enter. The six-panel Control Center screen appears (see fig. 1.3). (Your screen may display a variety of file names in the Control Center panels.) You now are ready to begin using dBASE IV.

```
  This software is licensed to:              Ashton-Tate
                                            Ashton-Tate
                                           Ashton-Tate
      A & M SERVICES, INC                  Ashton-Tate
      A & M SERVICES, INC                 Ashton-Tate
         0775835-35                      Ashton-Tate
                                        Ashton-Tate

   Copyright (c) 1986, 1988, 1990. Ashton-Tate Corporation. All
   Rights Reserved. dBASE, dBASE IV and Ashton-Tate are registered
   trademarks of Ashton-Tate Corporation.
   You may use the software and printed materials in the dBASE IV
   package under the terms of the Software License Agreement;
   please read it.  In summary, Ashton-Tate grants you a paid-up,
   non-transferable, personal license to use dBASE IV on one
   computer work station.  You do not become the owner of the
   package nor do you have the right to copy (except permitted
   backups of the software) or alter the software or printed
   materials.  You are legally accountable for any violation of the
   License Agreement and copyright, trademark, or trade secret law.

   Press ⏎ to assent to the License Agreement and begin dBASE IV
```

Fig. 1.2
The dBASE IV
copyright screen.

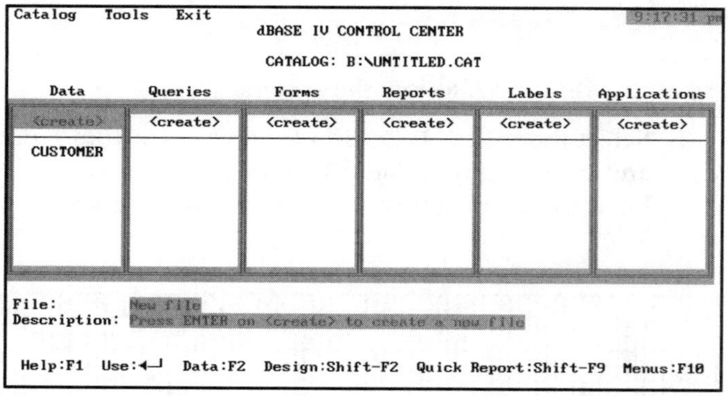

1

Fig. 1.3
The Control
Center screen.

```
Catalog   Tools   Exit                                          9:17:31 p
                           dBASE IV CONTROL CENTER
                          CATALOG: B:\UNTITLED.CAT

       Data        Queries       Forms       Reports      Labels    Applications
    <create>      <create>     <create>     <create>     <create>     <create>
    CUSTOMER



   File:        New file
   Description: Press ENTER on <create> to create a new file

   Help:F1  Use:◄┘  Data:F2  Design:Shift-F2  Quick Report:Shift-F9  Menus:F10
```

3. To activate a different work surface, verify that the cursor is on the word *Create* in the Data Panel and then press ◄Enter. The screen shown in figure 1.4 appears.

Objective 2: To Understand Menus and Work Surfaces

You can use the dBASE IV menu system to accomplish your database-management tasks. The menu system is a collection of work surfaces and menus. At the heart of the menu system is the *Control Center*. The Control Center is both a work surface and a menu that serves as a gateway to all dBASE IV's other work surfaces and menus. If you take time to understand the common work-surface features and to learn how to use the work surface and menus, you can reduce any anxiety you may have about learning dBASE IV.

When you work with the menu system in dBASE IV, your entire screen display can be considered a work surface. Technically, a *work surface* is the entire screen with the exception of any horizontal menu bar appearing at the top and any status bar, navigation line, and message line at the bottom.

Although the screens behind each Control Center panel are different, some common features make using all screens easy.

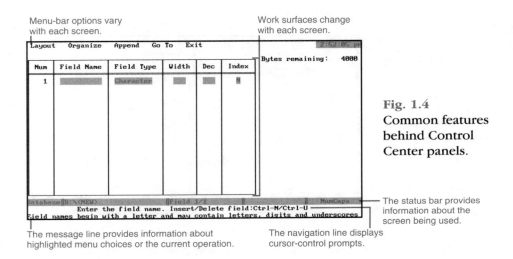

Menu-bar options vary with each screen.

Work surfaces change with each screen.

Fig. 1.4
Common features behind Control Center panels.

The status bar provides information about the screen being used.

The message line provides information about highlighted menu choices or the current operation.

The navigation line displays cursor-control prompts.

The Menu Bar

A menu bar appears in the top line of your screen, with its options arranged across the horizontal line. When you highlight a menu bar choice, a pull-down menu appears (see fig. 1.5).

Exercise 2.1: Accessing the Menu Bar

When the cursor is in the work-surface area, you can move the cursor to the menu bar in one of two ways:

1. Select the first option in the menu bar by pressing F10 .

    Alternatively, you can select any menu bar option directly by holding down Alt and pressing the first letter of the menu selection you want to choose.

2. After the cursor moves to the menu bar, press ← or → to move the cursor along the menu bar. A pull-down menu appears in a window just below the menu bar.

Accessing a Pull-Down Menu

The *pull-down menu*, sometimes called a *window*, contains a series of options arranged in a column. When any pull-down menu first appears, the first menu option is highlighted. A message appears in the lower portion of the screen explaining what the highlighted menu choice does.

1

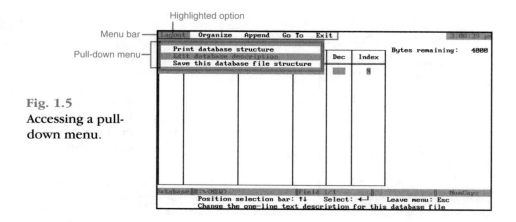

Fig. 1.5
Accessing a pull-
down menu.

Exercise 2.2: Choosing a Pull-Down Menu Option

To select a menu option from the pull-down menu, follow these steps:

1. Highlight any menu option by using ⬆ and ⬇. Then press ⏎Enter.
   Alternatively, you can press the first letter of a menu option. A different screen appears.

2. Press Esc. You are back to the pull-down menu.

3. Press Esc again to return to the previous work surface, the Data Design screen.

All menu bars include an Exit option. You must leave each menu bar by choosing this option if you want to save your work. If you press Esc, you lose your work.

The Status Bar

The status bar appears immediately below the work-surface area of the screen. The bar consists of a single row of five highlighted bars or sections (see fig. 1.6).

The status bar information (reading from left to right) includes the following sections:

* *Section 1:* Displays the current screen. The message Database, for example, appears when you are using a work surface to create fields in a database structure.

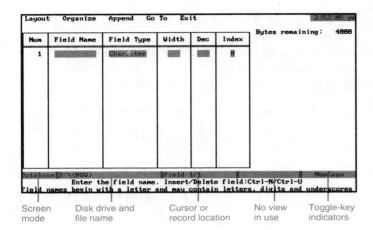

Fig. 1.6
The status bar.

- *Section 2:* Displays the current file and its path (the drive and directories).
- *Section 3:* Displays the cursor location or points to the current record, depending on the work surface in use.
- *Section 4:* Displays information about the file supplying data to the current operation.
- *Section 5:* Displays toggle-key status. *Toggle keys* are keys that you can press to turn an option on or off. Pressing a toggle key once may turn on an option, for example, and pressing the same key the second time turns off that option. (Ins), (Num Lock), and (Caps Lock) are examples of toggle keys. This status bar section can be blank, or any combination of the following toggle keys may appear:

    Num   Displays when you activate (Num Lock). This key (when activated) enables the numeric keypad to function as a simple calculator. When (Num Lock) is off, you can use numeric keypad arrow keys to move the cursor.

    Caps   Displays if you use (Caps Lock) to place in uppercase all the letter characters you type.

    Ins   Displays when you activate (Ins). When the screen is in Insert mode, on-screen text shifts to the right as you add new text.

You can turn off the status bar during certain tasks, such as editing. When the status bar is off, the toggle-key indicators appear in the top line of the screen. The status bar does not appear in the Control Center display.

1

The Navigation Line

The navigation line across the bottom of the screen displays information on how to perform activities such as moving the cursor or exiting a task (see fig. 1.7). Navigation information refers to the screen in use.

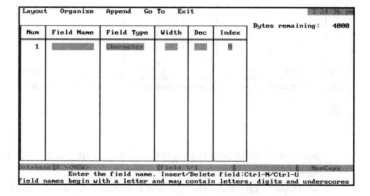

Fig. 1.7
The navigation
line.

This navigation line instructs you to enter a field name, press Ctrl + N to insert a field, or press Ctrl + U to delete the highlighted field.

The Message Line

Screens do not always contain a message line. If a message does appear, it provides instructions about the current operation and appears as the last line on-screen. The message line in figure 1.7 tells you how to format the field name when creating a database.

The general format of a dBASE IV screen display remains the same whether you are using the Data, Queries, Forms, Reports, Labels, or Applications features. The menu bar appears at the top; the status bar, navigation line, and message line display at the bottom; and the work surface occupies the remaining area.

Objective 3: To Use Keyboard Keys

You use many keys and key combinations to move around work surfaces and menus and to execute specific dBASE IV functions, but you do not need to memorize all the keys. Remember that you can find information about using the correct keys by looking at the navigation line. Keyboard layouts vary from one computer to another. Even though slight differences do occur, all keyboards have function keys, alphanumeric keys, cursor-movement keys, and numeric keys. Figure 1.8 shows the IBM Enhanced keyboard.

Function keys

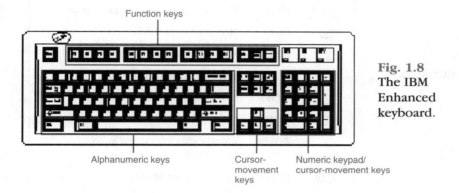

Fig. 1.8 The IBM Enhanced keyboard.

Alphanumeric keys

Cursor-
movement
keys

Numeric keypad/
cursor-movement keys

The Cursor-Control Keys

You use cursor-control keys to navigate within the work surface. The keys cause different movements or actions, depending on the work surface in use. If you press (Tab⇄) while you use the Edit screen work surface, for example, the cursor moves to the next field. Pressing (Tab⇄) while you are using Queries, however, moves the cursor to the next column. To be safe, always refer to the navigation line for instructions about the cursor-control keys that apply to the current action.

The Function Keys

Function keys appear on all keyboards. You may have a set of 10 function keys ((F1) through (F10)) on the left side of your keyboard, or you may have a set of 12 function keys ((F1) through (F12)) across the top of your keyboard. (Only the first 10 function keys are programmed to perform a specific task in dBASE IV. Pressing (F1) for example, activates on-screen Help.) The table of function keys shown in figure 1.9 provides a quick reference for using these keys.

You also can press each of the 10 function keys as you press (⇧Shift) to activate 10 additional programmed actions. Pressing (⇧Shift)+(F9), for example, accesses the Quick Report feature. The table of (⇧Shift)+*function keys* shown in figure 1.10 provides a quick reference for using these key combinations.

1

F1	HELP	Displays on-screen help
F2	DATA	Toggles between Browse and Edit screen display
F3	PREV	Moves to preceding field or page
F4	NEXT	Moves to next field or page
F5	FIELD	Adds or modifies a field
F6	SELECT	Selects contiguous text and fields
F7	MOVE	Moves selected text and fields
F8	COPY	Copies selected text and fields
F9	ZOOM	Enlarges/shrinks items such as Memo fields
F10	MENUS	Accesses menus for current screen

Fig. 1.9
Function keys.

The Menu Control Keys

Always keep in mind that what happens when you press a key can vary with your current position in the dBASE IV program. Figure 1.11 provides a reference for using menu control keys.

Exercise 3.1: Using the Keyboard

To become familiar with the keyboard, type the field data in the database Design screen. Follow these steps:

1. Position the cursor on the field name in line 1 of the Design screen. The status line should display Field 1/1.
2. Type Name in the field name area and press ↵Enter or Tab⇄.
3. Press ↵Enter to accept Character type for the field.
4. Type 15 for the width of the field and press ↵Enter.
5. Press ↵Enter to accept N in the Index field.

The cursor moves to line 2 of the Design screen. Use ←, →, ↓, or ↑ to go back to line 1 if you need to make any changes.

1

⇧Shift + F1	PICK	Displays list of items to choose from
⇧Shift + F2	DESIGN	Displays Design screen
⇧Shift + F3	FIND PREV	Finds last occurrence of search string
⇧Shift + F4	FIND NEXT	Locates next occurrence of search string
⇧Shift + F5	FIND	Finds search string
⇧Shift + F6	REPLACE	Replaces search string with another string
⇧Shift + F7	SIZE	Changes size of design and column width
⇧Shift + F8	DITTO	Carries data forward from corresponding field in preceding record
⇧Shift + F9	QUICKRPT	Prints Quick report of data in current database
⇧Shift + F10	MACRO	Calls macro prompt box

Fig. 1.10
⇧Shift +*function keys*.

Objective 4: To Use the Help Screens

dBASE IV offers three Help levels:

- Routine information display in navigation and message lines
- Automatic error-box display in certain problem situations
- User-activated, on-screen Help

17

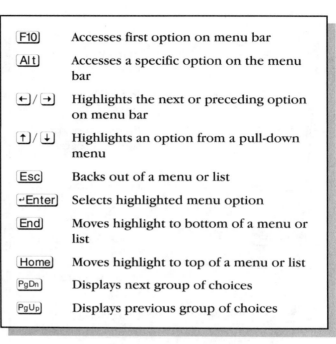

Fig. 1.11
Menu control
keys.

In all cases, Help is *context-sensitive*, which means that Help messages and screens refer to the task or command you are performing when you request Help.

Using Navigation and Message Line Help

You read about navigation and message lines earlier in this chapter. These lines in the lower portion of the screen are the first Help level and offer continuous information about the task you are performing. These lines require no action on your part; they simply are helpful instructions about actions you are taking and choices you can make.

Using Error Box Help

An error box appears when you make an error or incomplete entry. The boxed message names the error and offers options for correcting the problem.

1

Suppose that you attempt to execute a command that is not valid for what you are doing. You may get the message `Command Only Valid in Programs` in an error box, along with a display of the menu options Cancel, Edit, and Help. Cancel terminates the current operation so that you can begin again. Edit enables you to correct the erroneous entry and continue. Help calls a Help screen to provide you with additional information. To clear an error box from the screen, highlight your menu choice by using the arrow keys and press `⏎Enter`.

Exercise 4.1: Exiting dBASE without Saving

If you try to exit from your current operation without properly saving your work, dBASE IV automatically offers Help in the form of the error box message

    Are you sure you want to abandon operation?

To exit without saving, follow these steps:

1. Press `Esc` from the Design screen.

   The error box shown in figure 1.12 appears.

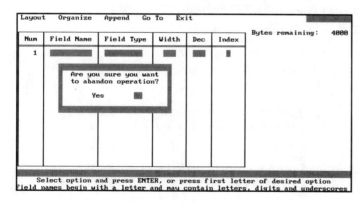

Fig. 1.12
An error box.

2. Select No as the menu choice to clear the error box message.

Exercise 4.2: Saving and Exiting the Database Structure

To be sure that you have saved the database structure before you exit, follow these steps:

1. Press `Alt`+`E` to activate the menu bar.

1

2. Select Save Changes and Exit by using ⬇ and pressing ↵Enter.
3. Type a file name (be sure to include the drive and directory). For example, type **a:sample** or **c:\db4\sample**.
4. Press ↵Enter.

You are returned to the Control Center.

Getting User-Activated Help

The Help box is a sophisticated context-sensitive Help system. After you press F1, you see a Help box that contains information about the current task.

Exercise 4.3: Using the Context-Sensitive Help Screen

Suppose that you see the Page Dimensions option on a Print menu and you don't understand what the option does. To activate a context-sensitive Help screen about the option, follow these steps:

1. Position the cursor on the database name SAMPLE and press ⬆Shift + F9 to activate the Quick Report feature.
2. Select the Page Dimensions option from the Print menu.
3. Press F1. The Help screen appears.
4. Use ←, →, ⬇, or ↑ to highlight menu choices at the bottom of the Help box (see fig. 1.13).

Fig. 1.13
The Help screen for the Page Dimensions option.

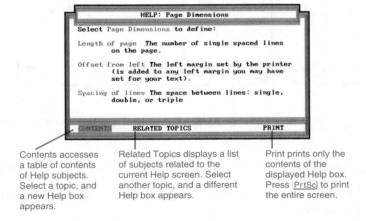

HELP: Page Dimensions

Select Page Dimensions to define:

Length of page   The number of single spaced lines
                  on the page.

Offset from left The left margin set by the printer
                  (is added to any left margin you may have
                  set for your text).

Spacing of lines The space between lines: single,
                  double, or triple

CONTENTS   RELATED TOPICS   PRINT

Contents accesses a table of contents of Help subjects. Select a topic, and a new Help box appears.

Related Topics displays a list of subjects related to the current Help screen. Select another topic, and a different Help box appears.

Print prints only the contents of the displayed Help box. Press PrtSc to print the entire screen.

5. Press ↵Enter to select the highlighted option.

20

As you begin to use dBASE IV, practice accessing the Help menu system. Press
(F1), select the Contents option, select a topic, and read the Help screen. If
you have a printer attached to your system, turn on the printer and print the
Help menu. When you are finished using a user-activated Help box, exit it by
pressing (Esc).

Objective 5: To Use Basic Print Options

Printing in dBASE IV is simple. Although you can print during many different
situations (described in later chapters), all printing is controlled by the same
Print menu.

You can access the Quick Reports feature to display the contents of a database
one record after another—in row and columnar format, for example. You also
can display data using a custom report format or a mailing label format.

In this section, you become familiar with the Print menu and its choices. Then
you learn the steps necessary to display records in a database by using the
Quick Report feature. In nearly every chapter that follows, you have an op-
portunity to use the Print menu to display data in one of dBASE IV's many
formats.

Understanding the Print Menu

Each time you print using dBASE IV, you use a common Print menu to control
the printing process (see fig. 1.14). dBASE IV has preset the selections on this
menu with commonly used defaults. Of course, after you become familiar with
the choices on the Print menu, you can exercise considerable control over
how your data is displayed. If you change the default settings on the Print
menu, you can even save these changes to disk and use them again.

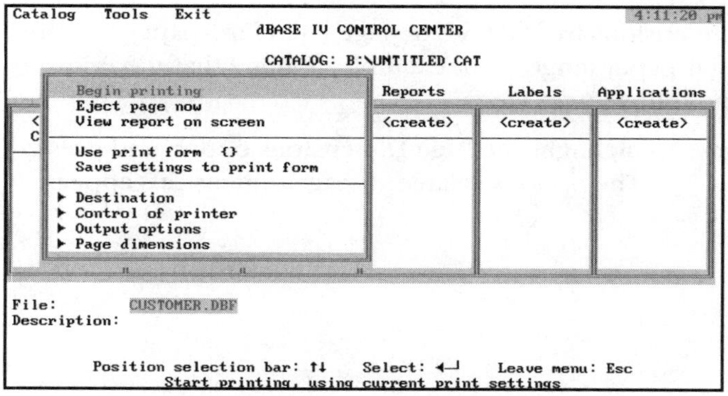

Fig. 1.14
The nine Print
menu options.

1

Your Print menu options follow:

- *Begin Printing:* Causes printing to begin, using currently set specifications. Press Ctrl+S to interrupt printing temporarily. Press Esc to
  stop printing entirely.

- *Eject Page Now:* Causes the printer to eject paper and begin printing
  at the top of the next page.

- *View Report on Screen:* Causes printing to appear on-screen. This
  option changes to View Labels when you access the Print menu from
  the Labels Design screen.

- *Use Print Form:* Causes a set of printer specifications stored on disk to
  be loaded and used when you print a file.

- *Save Settings to Print Form:* Causes the currently selected printer
  specifications to be saved to disk for later use.

- *Destination:* Causes output to be directed to a DOS file for later
  printing.

- *Control of Printer:* Determines the quality of printer output such as
  pitch (characters per inch), *page eject*, and *pausing between pages*
  (for single-sheet paper feeding). This option enables you to send
  special printer-control codes to the printer before and after printing.

- *Output Options:* Causes printing to begin and end on specified pages;
  indicates the number of copies.

- *Page Dimensions:* Determines paper size, left margin, and line
  spacing.

The first three options on the Print menu cause the appropriate action to be
taken. The remaining options cause pop-up menus to appear, from which you
must make other selections or type requested information.

Exercise 5.1: Changing Page Dimensions

To change the page dimensions from a 66-line page (standard-paper length)
to an 84-line page (legal-paper length), for example, assume that the Print
menu is on-screen, and follow these steps:

1. Use the arrow keys to highlight the Page Dimensions option and press
   ↵Enter (or press P). The options related to page dimensions appear
   (see fig. 1.15).

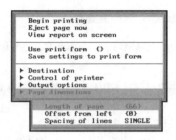

Fig. 1.15
Page dimension
options.

2. Use the arrow keys to highlight the Length of Page option and press
   ⏎Enter (or press L̲).

   A prompt to enter the new page length appears:

        Enter an integer:

3. Type 84 and press ⏎Enter at the prompt.

   At this point, you have changed the Print option and returned to the
   Print menu. Continue making changes until you are ready to print.
   When you are ready to print, select Begin Printing or View Report on
   Screen. You can understand this process more clearly by reading the
   following section on creating a Quick report.

Creating a Quick Report

The Quick Report feature provides a fast and simple way to print the current
database. All records in the current database are listed with each field appearing in a column. The field names chosen for the database serve as column
headings. Quick Report adds the page number and date to the top of each
page.

If the width of the record (a row in the report) is wider than your printer, the
excess print line *truncates* (cuts off) or wraps around to the next line, depending on your printer. Consult your printer manual for information about
how your printer handles lines that are too long to print.

Assume that you have created a file of customers that contains each person's
name, phone number, and amount owed.

23

Exercise 5.2: Printing a Quick Report

To print the contents of that file using dBASE IV's Quick Report feature, follow these steps:

1. Highlight the file name SAMPLE in the Control Center Data panel and press Shift+F9.

   Quick Report is activated, and the Print menu appears.

2. Select View Report on Screen to view the Quick report on your monitor, or select Begin Printing to send the report to the printer.

As you proceed through other chapters, the printing process will become more familiar, and you will begin to understand the versatility and ease of printing in dBASE IV.

Objective 6: To Navigate the Control Center

The Control Center, the gateway to most of dBASE IV's powerful features, has five parts, as shown in figure 1.16.

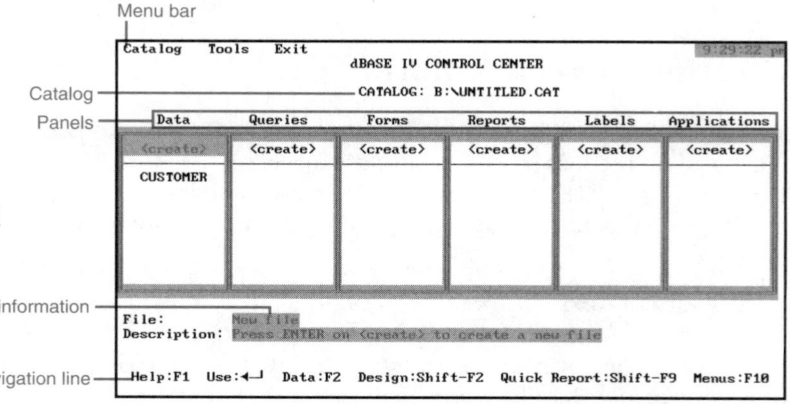

Fig. 1.16
The Control Center.

The *catalog* data listed above the six panels identifies the name of the active catalog. This Control Center feature is a dBASE IV technique for grouping related files. Using a catalog, you can store unrelated files in the same directory on a hard disk, yet keep the files separated into meaningful groups. Only files listed in the open catalog can be displayed in the Control Center panels. If you do not open a catalog to keep track of the files you are using, dBASE IV automatically opens a catalog called UNTITLED.CAT.

1

Two *file information* lines display the file name and description of the highlighted file. The *navigation line* at the bottom of the screen identifies the most commonly used Control Center function keys. The Control Center *panels* and the *menu bar* are explained in the following two sections.

Using the Control Center Panels

Six panels represent the dBASE operations you perform through the Control Center. You can create and maintain databases (Data panel); design searches and views to access the data you want (Queries panel); create custom screens (Forms panel), custom reports (Reports panel), and custom labels (Labels panel); and write custom programs (Applications panel).

The first entry in each panel is Create. A line appears under the Create option. Under the line, you see a listing of any files associated with the specific panel. To access a panel, use ⬅, ➡, ⬇, or ⬆. To highlight a file within a panel, use the arrow keys.

To select the Create option to establish a new file, highlight Create and press ⏎Enter. To use an existing file, select the file name and press ⏎Enter. After you select a file name, it moves above the horizontal line in the panel.

Using the Control Center Menu Bar

The Control Center menu bar contains three options: Catalog, Tools, and Exit. These menus enable you to control the organization of your files, to access a variety of utility operations, and to exit dBASE IV.

The Catalog choice on the Control Center menu bar offers options for managing your dBASE IV files (see fig. 1.17). The first option on the Catalog menu enables you to select a different catalog. The Catalog menu also contains options enabling you to add and remove files from the current catalog or to change the name and description of the catalog or its files. To access the Catalog menu, press F10 or Alt+C.

Use ⬅, ➡, ⬇, or ⬆ to highlight the Catalog menu option you want, and then press ⏎Enter.

The Tools option on the Control Center menu bar enables you to access DOS commands, import data from (or export data to) software programs other than dBASE, set up macros (capturing keystrokes for reuse), use passwords to protect data, and use a number of more advanced features. To access the Tools menu, press F10 or Alt+T.

Use ⬅, ➡, ⬇, or ⬆ to highlight the Tools menu option you want, and then press ⏎Enter.

1

Fig. 1.17
Choosing an
option from the
Catalog menu.

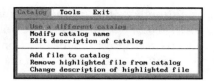

Catalog	Tools	Exit
Use a different catalog
Modify catalog name
Edit description of catalog
Add file to catalog
Remove highlighted file from catalog
Change description of highlighted file

Objective 7: To Exit dBASE IV

Never turn off your computer before properly exiting dBASE IV. Failing to exit
properly could result in damaged files.

Exercise 7.1: Exiting dBASE IV

To exit dBASE IV, follow these steps:

1. Return to the six-panel Control Center, if you are not there.
2. Press F10 and select the Exit option. Alternatively, you can press
   Alt + E. Two exit options appear.
3. Select Quit to DOS and then press ↵Enter.

Using the Exit option ensures that you leave dBASE IV properly. If you do not
use the Exit option, you risk damaging your files and wasting hours of work.

Chapter Summary

This chapter provided an overview of the operating environment of dBASE IV.
If you take the time to understand the variety of screen displays provided by
the program, you will find it easier to perform database management activities.
In the next chapter, you design and create a database.

Testing Your Knowledge

True/False Questions

1. The menu system is a collection of work surfaces and menus.
2. The status bar appears immediately above the work-surface area of the
   screen.

3. All 12 function keys perform specific tasks in dBASE IV.

4. An error box appears when you make an error or incomplete entry.

5. The Control Center, the gateway to most of dBASE IV's powerful features, has five parts.

Multiple Choice Questions

1. At the heart of the menu system is the
   - A. work surface.
   - B. control panel.
   - C. Control Center.
   - D. menu bar.
   - E. status bar.

2. The status bar, which appears below the work surface area of the screen, does not display the
   - A. screen type.
   - B. cursor location.
   - C. disk drive and file name.
   - D. page number.
   - E. toggle-key indicators.

3. To activate the Quick Report feature,
   - A. press [Alt]+[F9].
   - B. press [⇧Shift]+[F9].
   - C. press [F9].
   - D. press [F2].
   - E. press [F10].

4. The Control Center menu contains the three options
   - A. Catalog, Utilities, and Exit.
   - B. Reports, Catalog, and Exit.
   - C. Catalog, Tools, and Save.
   - D. Catalog, Tools, and Exit.
   - E. Directory, Tools, and Quit.

1

5. To exit dBASE IV, from the Control Center,
    A. press F10, select the Exit Option, and select Quit to DOS.
    B. press Alt + E and select Quit to DOS.
    C. press F10 and select Exit to DOS.
    D. press Alt + S and select Exit.
    E. both A and B.

Fill-in-the-Blank Questions

1. The menu system is collection of _____ surfaces and
    _____.
2. The _____ menu, sometimes called a *window*, contains a series of options arranged in a column.
3. The _____ line across the bottom of the screen displays information on how to perform activities.
4. The boxed error message names the _____ and offers _____ for correcting the problem.
5. Using the Quick Report feature, all _____ in the current database are listed with each _____ appearing in a column.

Review: Short Projects

1. Accessing and Moving around in dBASE IV

    Enter the dBASE program, and in the Control Center, practice moving from one panel to another using the arrow keys and Tab. Activate the menu bar and select Quit to DOS.

2. Entering Field Names

    From the Control Center, select Create from the data panel. Type two field names: ACCTNO, Character, 5 and Name, character, 15. Print the structure. Exit without saving.

3. Listing Menu Options and Keyboard Keys

    List the menu options and keyboard keys from the Control Center to design a new database, save the structure, and exit dBASE IV.

Review: Long Projects

1
1. Entering Fields and Exiting without Saving

    Select Create from the data panel. Enter the following two fields:

Field Name	LOCATION	EVENT
Field type	character	character
Field width	15	10

    Press [Esc] and print the screen error message. Exit the Design screen without saving. Press [F1] and print the screen with the Help message. Exit dBASE IV.

2. Entering Three Fields and Saving before Exiting

    From the Control Center, select Create from the data panel. Type three fields:

Field name	NAME	MAJOR	COURSE
Field type	character	character	character
Field width	15	5	20

    Save the database structure as STUDENT.

Designing and Creating a Database

You can maintain a powerful database in computer memory. You must remember, however, that the computer is only a machine—it cannot work for you without structure and rules. The rules for its use vary from one program to another. If you type the phone number **123-4567** in a word processing program, for example, the number appears just as you typed it. If you type the same number into a spreadsheet program, however, you see the number -4444. A spreadsheet interprets the hyphen as a minus sign and subtracts the last four digits from the first three digits. Obviously, you must take the time to learn the rules of each program you use. As you will discover, the rules in dBASE IV, a database management system, can be learned gradually and used effectively.

The first step in implementing a electronic database management system should be to design the database on paper, based on in-depth discussions with prospective users of the system. This chapter discusses database design techniques and the dBASE IV rules to follow when you create a database structure.

Objectives

2

1. To Design a Database
2. To Create the Database Structure
3. To Save the Database Structure
4. To Edit and Print the Database Structure

Key Terms Used in This Chapter	
ASCII	A standard set of characters, which includes the letters, numbers, and other symbols available on your keyboard, such as a dollar sign ($) and an asterisk (*).
Field	A specific type of data, such as a part number or a unit cost.
Record	A collection of related fields. All fields (such as Part Number, Description, Unit Cost, and Primary Vendor in an inventory, for example) concerned with one item constitute a record.
Database	A collection of related records, such as the information about all items in an inventory, for example.
Catalog	The mechanism in dBASE IV to group the user's related database file names.
Index	A way to display or print database contents in a specified order. Use one index, for example, to list inventory records sorted by primary vendor; use another index to list the same records sorted by part number.

Objective 1: To Design a Database

The human mind retains a collection of facts and assumptions, which it organizes by using a set of intuitive rules. Most of the time, this process works just fine. When you need to share a vast amount of information with many people, however, you will find the electronic database management system a very useful tool.

2

To design, create, and maintain a database requires transferring intuitive rules to a database management program. You should resist the urge to sit down at the keyboard and begin creating the database structure before you plan carefully what you want to do with the data.

Suppose that you want to create a database to track vehicle sales to customers of a car dealership. You can think of obvious parts (fields) to include in your database. A customer database obviously would include fields of names, addresses, vehicle descriptions, and amounts charged. Yet other not-so-obvious fields may come to mind if you thoroughly analyze what you want your database to do. You could include in the database a Last Purchase Date field, for example, which would trigger the mailing of promotional material to customers who had failed to make a purchase in the last three years. Some useful techniques can make planning easy and help you avoid omitting important items.

Setting the Database Objective

After consulting with end users of the proposed database, write a clear and concise objective statement that describes the purpose of the database. That's all; try not to describe specific data items or output reports. Consider including who will use the data, what information needs must be met, and how timely the data must be. Figure 2.1 shows an example of an objective statement. Circulate the objective statement to end users for modifications and final approval.

New Car Sales Database
Statement of Objectives:

Develop an information system that will provide management with new car sales information specific to each customer. Provide contact information and follow-up contact list; provide the service department with a record of warranty work performed on new cars that includes customer contact information. Information is collected by sales persons at the time of sale or the service writer at the time of service. Information is available in the information system within 48 hours.

Fig. 2.1
Database Design
Tip #1: Clarify the
purpose of the
database with a
written objective
statement.

2

Analyzing the Current System

If you already are using a paper or computer database system, use that as a starting point. A system already in place can indicate what information, expected outputs, and data fields you must have in your dBASE IV database. Your task may be as simple as automating a manual system with dBASE IV or converting from an old computer or outdated software to dBASE IV. Begin your dBASE IV application error-free by making sure that your old system does what you want before you use it as the basis for your database design. If the old system doesn't meet your needs, you probably should redesign the system from scratch.

Describing Desired Outputs

The easiest way to know what data fields should be in a database system is to figure out what the end users want the database to produce. First, determine what lists, reports, and labels are needed. Writing a brief objective statement about each output can be helpful (see fig. 2.2).

Fig. 2.2
Database Design
Tip #2: Determine
desired outputs
before choosing
input fields for
a proposed
database.

New Car Sales Database

1. Sales Recap
   Report

   List all new car sales for the month, organized by sales person and date of delivery. Subtotal by sales person and grand total at end of report. Include vehicle identification number, date of delivery, price paid, trade-in yes/no, and first-time buyer yes/no for each car sold.

2. Customer List

   List all customers, arranged alphabetically by last then first name. Include customer last name, first name, address, city, state, ZIP code, and phone number.

3. Index Card
   Labels

   List all customers, arranged by sales person, by customer's last name and first name. Include Customer's last name, first name, address, city, state, ZIP code, and phone number.

Designing Output Layouts

Take the time to sketch the format of the desired lists, reports, and labels. Think about the order in which the information should appear, what totals and subtotals are necessary, and which database records are needed. Figure 2.3 shows some sample sketches. The layouts help the database developer to visualize the required data fields and lessen the likelihood that important fields will be omitted.

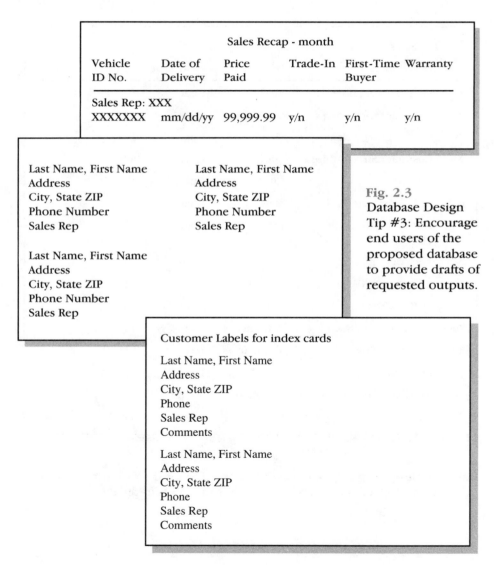

Fig. 2.3
Database Design Tip #3: Encourage end users of the proposed database to provide drafts of requested outputs.

Establishing a Data Dictionary

Based on the type and width of data items appearing in output layouts, prepare a written list—called a *data dictionary*—of each data field that should be in the new database (see fig. 2.4). Include a field name, description of data, type of data, size of field, number of decimal places, and an indication of whether the field is to be used for ordering (indexing) items. Update the data dictionary as changes are made.

New Car Sales Data Dictionary

No.	Description	Field Name	Field Type	Width	Dec	Index
1	Vehicle ID Number	Vin	Char	10		X
2	Customer Last Name	Last Name	Char	15		
3	Customer First Name	First Name	Char	10		
4	Customer Street Address	Address	Char	30		
5	Customer City	City	Char	15		
6	Customer State Code	State	Char	2		
7	Customer ZIP Code (10 digits)	ZIP	Char	10		
8	Price of Car	Car_Price	Num	8	2	
9	Sales Rep Initials	Sales_Rep	Char	3		
10	Delivery Date	Date_Del	Date	8		
11	Warranty Purchased	Warranty	Log	1		
12	Trade-In Allowed	Trade_In	Log	1		
13	First-Time Buyer	First_Buy	Log	1		
14	Sales Rep Comments	Comments	Memo	10		
15	Phone	Phone	Char	14		

Fig. 2.4
Database Design Tip #4: Develop documentation for the proposed database in the form of a data dictionary that describes all fields in the database.

dBASE IV sets certain restrictions for using fields as indexes and for entering the field names, field types, field widths, and decimal places shown in the data dictionary.

Choosing a Field Name

Choose a name for each standard data item (field) in your database. You need these names to refer to data stored in fields when you use the Control Center's work surfaces. Names may have from 1 to 10 characters and may contain letters, numbers, and the underscore character. The first character in your field name must be a letter, however.

Although N is a valid name for a field, using a single-character name makes it difficult to remember what type of data the field contains. Try to choose a field name that describes the data in the field. You also may want to insert an underscore to increase the usefulness of a name. You may name the inventory part number field INV_NUM rather than INVNUM, for example. Do not include any blank spaces.

Choosing a Field Type

The field type tells dBASE IV the classification of data stored in the field. You can choose one of six data types: Character, Numeric, Float, Date, Logical, or Memo. Use Character as the field type if the field type contains both numeric and alphabetic characters. The field types are as follows:

- *Character*. Use this data type for all combinations of numeric and alphabetic data.
- *Numeric*. Use this data type for all numbers to be used in calculations (except for those numbers described in the Float data type).

  Note: If data looks numeric but is not used in calculations (phone number, ZIP code, or Social Security number, for example), use the Character data type.
- *Float*. Use this data type for scientific applications that use very large or small numbers that are frequently multiplied. Also use Float for a number containing five or more digits or decimal places, such as pi or the speed of light.
- *Date*. Use this data type for all dates.

2

- *Logical*. Use this data type for fields that contain a value representing True or False. You can type the value as upper- or lowercase—T (True), F (False), Y (Yes), or N (No). You may keep an out-of-stock (Yes or No) field in an inventory database, for example, in order to maintain an up-to-date listing of unavailable items.

- *Memo*. Use this data type to attach narrative about the current record when you do not want to limit (other than the inevitable limit of available memory) the amount of the data in the field. The other five field types have width constraints on content (discussed in the next section). If you have to submit a person's credit record, for example, you are required to maintain a 500-word rebuttal. The Memo type is ideal for this data.

Specifying a Field Width

Use the field width specification to indicate the maximum number of characters or digits a field can hold. You must specify widths for Character, Numeric, and Float fields; dBASE supplies the widths for the Date, Logical, and Memo fields. Following are the length requirements:

- *Character*. Enter a field width as narrow as 1 or as wide as 254. Field content can include any ASCII character.

- *Numeric and Float*. Enter a field width between 1 and 20.

- *Date and Logical*. dBASE IV supplies a Date field width of 8 and a Logical field width of 1. Dates appear in the format mm/dd/yy (month/day/year), such as 01/24/92.

- *Memo*. dBASE IV supplies a field width of 10. Although the field in the record displays only the word Memo, dBASE IV can store a large document at another location.

Specifying Decimal Places in the Field

You must indicate the number of decimal places (Dec) for two types of fields: Numeric and Float. The number of decimal places must be at least two less than the specified width of the field. If the largest unit price in your inventory record is 8 digits (6 digits and 2 decimal places), for example, set the width to 10 to reserve space for a period and a sign.

Establishing a Field as an Index

Place a **Y** in the Index column to mark the corresponding field as one on which to organize records for display to screen or printer. When describing an inventory database, for example, you can specify Yes in the Index column for the description field if you plan to print reports showing inventory listed alphabetically by description. dBASE IV supports up to 47 indexes per database.

Establishing a Cross-Reference Document

Based on the appearance of data fields in output layouts, prepare a written list, or *cross-reference*, in the following format:

- Across the page, list all planned outputs to the screen and to the printer.
- Down the side, list all data fields.

Next to each data field, check which reports use each field's content. If someone suggests a change to the database structure, the cross-reference document makes it easy to assess the effect of the proposed change on the established database outputs. Figure 2.5 shows a sample cross-reference document for a database.

Now you are ready to create the database structure according to the specifications documented in the data dictionary. One final word of warning: resist the "everything but the kitchen sink" approach of building in more data than you need. Extra data takes up space, makes the system run slower, and costs money to maintain.

Don't worry if you have to adjust the original design specifications. With dBASE IV, you can add, delete, and change data fields whenever necessary and with little effort.

Objective 2: To Create the Database Structure

After you complete the extensive database design activities, creating the database structure is primarily a matter of typing. You must access the dBASE IV program, specify the default disk drive and path where the database is to be stored, choose a catalog, choose Create from the Control Center Data panel, enter up to five items of information about each field, and then save the database structure.

2

New Car Sales Data and Report Cross Reference

Field Name	Sales Recap	Customer List	Customer Label
Vin	X		
Last Name		X	X
First Name		X	X
Address		X	X
City	X	X	
State	X	X	
ZIP	X	X	
Car_Price	X		
Sales_Rep	X		
Date_Del	X		
Warranty	X		
Trade_In	X		
First_Buy	X		
Comments			X
Phone		X	X

Fig. 2.5
Database Design Tip #5: Develop a cross-reference document that shows
which fields are included in each planned output for the proposed database.

Specifying the Default Disk and Directory

Your system probably has several disk drives, one of which is a hard disk with
many directories. Before you create or use a database, you must tell dBASE IV
the location of the database and associated files. You need to point to the
appropriate storage location only once at the beginning of an editing session.

Exercise 2.1: Setting the Default Directory

Establishing the location of the database files is important if dBASE is to save the file to your disk. The default directory is the directory where dBASE saves or retrieves your files.

To set the default directory to drive B, follow these steps:

1. To access dBASE IV, select the dBASE IV option from your Custom menu, or type **dbase** and press ⏎Enter. The Control Center appears.

2. Press Alt + T to select the Tools menu (see fig. 2.6).

   By using the Tools menu, you can access many utility operations: importing and exporting data, creating macros, initiating DOS operations from within dBASE IV, setting passwords, and changing dBASE IV settings that control the behavior of the software.

   Alternatively, you can press F10, select Tools, and press ⏎Enter. Throughout the remainder of the book, only the Alt + *letter* method of accessing menu bar choices is given.

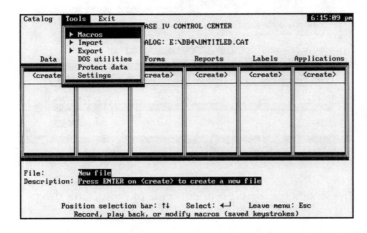

Fig. 2.6
The Tools menu.

3. Press D to select the DOS Utilities menu (see fig. 2.7).

4. Press Alt + D to select DOS.

5. Press S to select Set Default Drive:Directory (see fig. 2.8).

   This option displays the current default and enables you to enter a different disk drive and directory for dBASE IV to use in creating or accessing database files.

2

Fig. 2.7
Using the DOS
Utilities menu to
perform DOS
functions from
within dBASE IV.

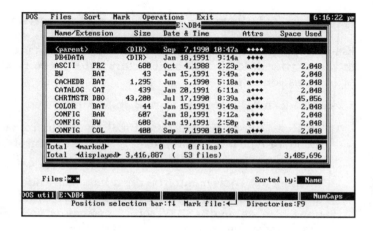

Fig. 2.8
Selecting the
Set Default
Drive:Directory
option.

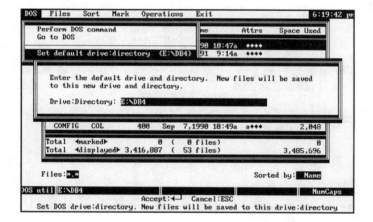

6. Press Del until dBASE deletes the current contents of the default drive or directory.

7. Type the name of the disk drive and directory in the Drive:Directory field (in this case, a:\ or b:\) and then press ↵Enter (see fig. 2.9).

Typing this specification tells dBASE IV to store and access database files on drive A or B in the root directory.

8. Press Alt+E to select the Exit option, and then press ↵Enter to return to the Control Center.

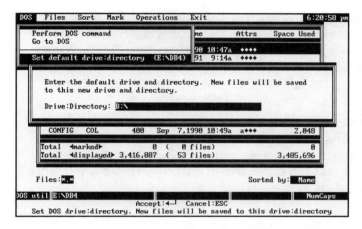

Fig. 2.9
Specifying the
disk drive and
directory.

After entering the default disk drive and directory, you return to the Control Center. Above the Control Center panels, you see a message in the catalog name area that includes the drive you just specified—in this case, CATALOG: B:\UNTITLED.CAT. After you set the default drive and directory, you can choose to create a catalog.

Choosing a Catalog

Before specifying a new database structure, you may choose a catalog to keep track of files that are related. In the standard library coding system, all related books are grouped in a section (or catalog). Perhaps you just want to browse for a particular type of book, such as poetry or history, or you cannot remember the author or title of a cookbook. You do know that you can find all poetry works in one section (catalog), all history books in another section, and all cookbooks in a third area.

Think of the disk directory that contains your dBASE IV files as a library. You should use the catalog capability if you are likely to have a number of unrelated databases, each with its own set of reports, labels, and so on. (If you do not use the catalog feature, dBASE IV puts all files that you create in a catalog called UNTITLED.) To create or select a catalog, use the Catalog option on the menu bar in the Control Center.

43

Exercise 2.2: Creating a New Catalog

Catalogs also can be thought of as books and your database files as chapters. You may want to keep related database files, all with unique file names, in one location. This location is the catalog. To create a new catalog, follow these steps:

1. Press [Alt]+[C] from the Control Center to access the Catalog pull-down menu (see fig. 2.10).

   With the Catalog pull-down menu, you can create or change catalogs, rename a catalog, add and delete files in the current catalog, or change a catalog or file description.

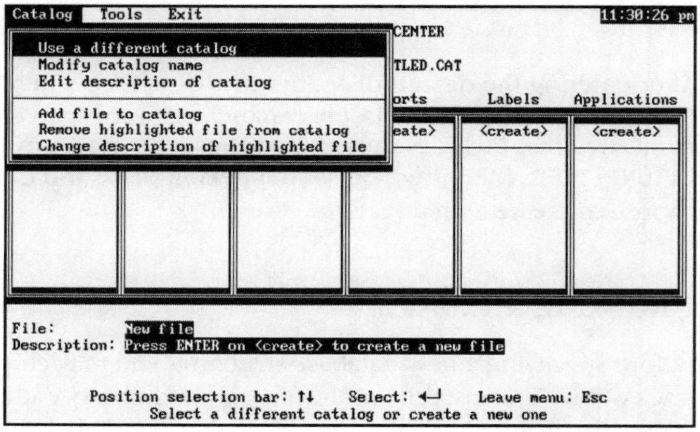

Fig. 2.10
The Catalog pull-down menu.

```
Catalog  Tools  Exit                                        11:30:26 pm
┌─────────────────────────────────────┐ CENTER
│ Use a different catalog              │
│ Modify catalog name                 │ TLED.CAT
│ Edit description of catalog          │
│                                     │ rts      Labels      Applications
│ Add file to catalog                 │
│ Remove highlighted file from catalog │ ate>    <create>    <create>
│ Change description of highlighted file│
└─────────────────────────────────────┘


File:       New file
Description: Press ENTER on <create> to create a new file

      Position selection bar: ↑↓    Select: ←┘    Leave menu: Esc
              Select a different catalog or create a new one
```

2. Select the option Use a Different Catalog from the Catalog menu.

   The Catalog picklist appears in the upper right corner of the screen (see fig. 2.11). The picklist presents an option to create a new catalog or enables you to use an existing catalog by highlighting a displayed choice and pressing [←Enter].

3. Select Create from the Catalog picklist and press [←Enter]. The Enter Name of New Catalog prompt appears.

4. At the prompt, type the name of catalog to be created. Type **lesson** and press [←Enter].

The Control Center screen reappears, and dBASE displays the catalog name LESSON above the panels.

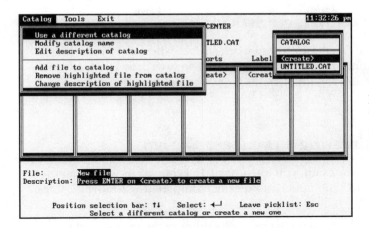

Fig. 2.11
The Catalog
picklist.

To select an existing catalog, choose the name of the catalog from the picklist. The catalog you create or select becomes the current catalog. Any files or forms you create will appear in the current catalog. Similarly, you see and access only file names in the current catalog. You can create as many catalogs as you need to organize your database files.

Accessing the Database Design Work Surface

After you create or select a catalog, you must access the Database Design work surface in order to create a new database structure.

Exercise 2.3: Accessing the Design Work Surface

You enter the names, types, and sizes of the fields in the Database Design work surface. To access that surface, follow these steps:

1. Access the Control Center screen.
2. Highlight Create in the Data control panel and press ⏎Enter). (Or press ⇧Shift] + F2].)

dBASE IV positions the cursor in the Field Name column. Each row in the Database Design work surface represents a field in a database record.

2

Specifying Field Characteristics

When you access the Database Design work surface, the cursor rests in the Field Name column next to the number 1. You are ready to specify in your database structure the field names that you documented in the data dictionary.

Exercise 2.4: Creating a Database Design

To create the database design, you must have determined the field names, type, and size. To enter the fields into dBASE, complete the following steps for each field:

1. Type the field names from figure 2.12, beginning with **vin**, and press ⏎Enter to move the cursor to the Field Type column.

2. Press ⏎Enter to choose the default Character field type. (You also can press the space bar until the appropriate data type appears and press ⏎Enter.)

3. Type the desired width of the field—for example, **10**—and press ⏎Enter.

   This step is necessary only if you used the Character, Numeric, or Float field type.

4. Type the number of decimal places for the field and press ⏎Enter.

   This step is necessary only if you used the Numeric or Float field type.

5. Press ⏎Enter to accept the default No setting in the Index column or press Y (Yes) and press ⏎Enter to establish the field as one on which to order data sent to the screen or printer.

Remember that dBASE follows these rules:

- Field names must start with a letter and are limited to 10 characters (letters, numbers, and underscores).

- dBASE IV supports six field types: Character, Numeric, Float, Date, Logical, or Memo.

- dBASE assigns widths for three field types: Date (8), Logical (1), and Memo (10). Include a space for a decimal point and one for a sign when you specify Numeric or Float field widths.

Continue to type field characteristics until you have defined all data fields. Review the entries in your structure and correct any errors you find. Figure 2.12 shows an example of field specifications for a vehicle sales database.

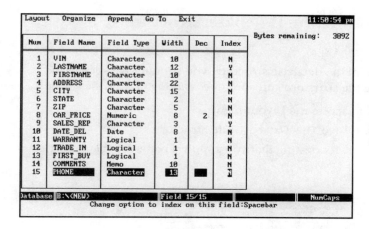

Fig. 2.12
Field specifications
for a vehicle sales
database.

Also keep the following guidelines in mind as you enter or edit fields on the
Database Design work surface:

- Press ← or → to move the cursor within a field. If the cursor is at
  the beginning of a field when you press ← or at the end of a field
  when you press →, the cursor moves to the preceding or next field,
  respectively.

- Press ↑ or ↓ to move up or down one field description.

- For efficiency's sake, fields used for indexing should be near the
  beginning of the record.

- Press Tab↹ or ⇧Shift + Tab↹ to move the cursor to the next or
  preceding field, respectively.

- Make any corrections by pressing Ins or Del.

- Press Ctrl + N to insert a field at the cursor location or Ctrl + U to
  delete the current field.

Objective 3: To Save the Database Structure

After creating the database structure, you can save your new database structure and continue to edit the structure. Alternatively, you can save the structure and exit to the Control Center.

47

Exercise 3.1: Saving the Database Structure without Exiting

As you type portions of the database structure, you should save your work periodically. To save the structure and continue working, follow these steps:

1. Press [Alt]+[L] to access the Layout menu.

2. Select the option Save This Database File Structure.

   A prompt appears, requesting that you supply a name for the database structure (see fig. 2.13).

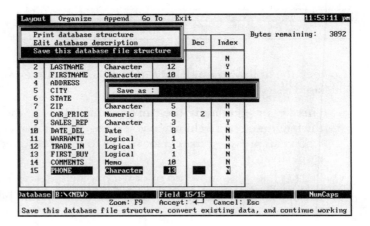

Fig. 2.13
Saving the database structure.

3. Type a file name; for example, type cars.

4. Press [↵Enter]. (The Database Design screen remains on-screen in this example, but the file name in the status bar changes from NEW to CARS to indicate that the new structure has been placed on disk.)

Exercise 3.2: Saving and Exiting the Database Structure

When you exit the database, you should save the work you have completed. To save the CARS structure and exit to the Control Center, follow these steps:

1. Press [Alt]+[E] to access the Exit menu.

2. Select Save Changes and Exit.

3. Type a file name and press [↵Enter] if prompted to do so.

Exercise 3.3: Exiting without Saving the Database Structure

At times you may find that you have made unwanted changes to the database or that you are dissatisfied with the ways you have changed the database. Just exit the current structure without saving your work. Then you can retrieve the original database, not the erroneous one. To exit without saving your changes, follow these steps:

1. Select Exit from the menu bar. The Exit menu then appears.

2. Select Abandon Changes and Exit. The Control Center then appears.

Closing the Database

When you finish using the database, you must instruct dBASE IV to close the database. Only one database will appear open on the Control Center Data panel. The name of the open database appears above the horizontal dividing line in the Data panel on the Control Center work surface. The names of closed databases appear below the line.

Exiting dBASE IV properly through the Control Center or opening another database closes the current open database. A good practice is to close a database when it is not in use. Under certain circumstances, an open database can be damaged by a power failure, a power surge, or by inadvertently performing a warm boot.

Closing the Database

Exiting dBASE automatically closes all databases, but you should form a habit of closing each database after you complete your work in it. To close an open database, follow these steps:

1. Select the database name—for example, CARS—in the Data panel.

2. Press ⏎Enter.

3. Select Close File and press ⏎Enter.

Objective 4: To Edit and Print the Database Structure

2

Rarely is a database structure perfect when you first enter it. Therefore, editing is an important part of working with dBASE.

Regardless of the work that you are doing with a structure—creating or modifying it, you should print a copy of the structure so that you have a working copy for documentation.

Modifying the Database Structure

Many times you will need to modify a database structure. You may find a design error, for example, such as a field size that is too narrow to hold the required data. Sometimes you may need to add another field. You can edit a database structure easily—even after data is stored in the database.

Exercise 4.1: Changing the Database Structure

To access a database structure, make changes, and save the changes, follow these steps:

1. Select the database name, CARS, in the Data panel.

2. Press ⚬Shift + F2 to access the Database Design work surface (see fig. 2.14).

   Alternatively, you can press ↵Enter, select Modify Structure/Order, and then press ↵Enter.

Fig. 2.14
The structure you chose in the background of the work surface with the Organize pull-down menu in the foreground.

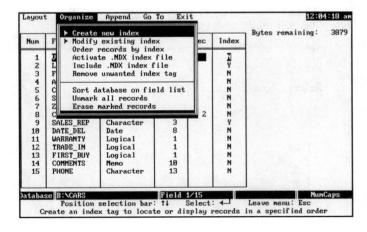

3. Press [Esc] to clear the Organize pull-down menu and access a full-screen display of the Database Design work surface.

4. Use the cursor keys to access the fields to be changed, and enter the changes if you made an error.

5. Select Exit from the menu bar, and select Save Changes and Exit.

Printing the Database Structure

If you have returned to the Control Center, you must access the Database Design work surface to print the structure. The process is simple.

Exercise 4.2: Printing the Database Structure

To print the database structure, follow these steps:

1. Press [Alt]+[L] to access the Layout option on the menu bar of the Database Design work surface.

2. Select Print Database Structure from the Layout pull-down menu.

3. Select Begin Printing from the Print menu.

   The printed database structure looks very similar to the structure viewed on the Database Design work surface.

4. Press [Alt]+[E] to access Exit, press [S] to select Save Changes and Exit, and then press [↵Enter].

You can stop the printer temporarily by pressing [Ctrl]+[S]. Press [Esc] to cancel a print operation.

Chapter Summary

This chapter explained basic database design techniques and illustrated the activities associated with creating a dBASE IV database structure. The chapter stressed the importance of planning the design of the database, using catalogs, and the ease in changing the design. In Chapter 3, you learn how to add and edit records in the database.

Testing Your Knowledge

True/False Questions

1. After completing the extensive database design activities, creating the database structure is primarily a matter of typing.

2. After you set the default drive and directory, you must create a catalog.

3. When you access the Database Design work surface, the cursor rests in the field name column next to number 2.

4. Field names must start with a letter and are limited to 10 characters—including letters, numbers, and underscores.

5. The name of the closed database appears above the horizontal dividing line in the Data panel on the Control Center work surface.

Multiple Choice Questions

1. A database design tip is to
    A. design a flowchart.
    B. write an algorithm.
    C. provide drawings of requested output.
    D. design a grammatical dictionary.
    E. design a new system even if an old system exists.

2. Field types do not include the
    A. Numeric type.
    B. Float type.
    C. Character type.
    D. Alphanumeric type.
    E. Date type.

3. An example of a catalog feature is
    A. keeping all class rosters in a catalog called CLASS.
    B. keeping all files in an untitled area.
    C. keeping each file under a unique catalog name.
    D. keeping all books in a library in the individual topic catalogs.
    E. both A and B.

4. dBASE assigns widths for three field types:

    A. Date, Character, and Numeric.

    B. Date, Logical, and Memo.

    C. Character, Date, and Logical.

    D. Numeric, Character, and Decimal.

    E. Numeric, Date, and Memo.

5. Exiting dBASE IV properly through the Control Center or opening another database

    A. keeps the current database open.

    B. closes the current open database.

    C. keeps up to three databases open at one time.

    D. automatically closes every database after you exit to the Control Center.

    E. keeps the database open when you enter dBASE IV the next time.

Fill-in-the-Blank Questions

1. To _____, _____, and _____ a database requires transferring intuitive rules to a database management program.

2. A written list of each data field that should be in the new database is called a _____.

3. Use the _____ data type for all numbers to be used in calculations.

4. You create or select a catalog using the _____ option on the menu bar in the Control Center.

5. In order to change a design error, such as an incorrect field size, you need to _____ the database structure.

Review: Short Projects

1. Designing a File

Using the five design tips, design a student file that will produce a list of students—including Social Security number, name, course, grade, and semester. Also design a report that will produce a list of students that have courses in common.

2

2. Creating a Catalog

Create a catalog called CLASS. Create the database design structure in Project 1, and save it as STUDENT.

3. Modifying a Database Structure

Modify the dBASE structure in Project 2, adding two fields: item number for the course and the instructor. Print the database structure.

Review: Long Projects

1. Documenting a Database

Using the design tips, document a database for a store inventory. Be able to produce reports with item numbers, product codes, descriptions, quantities, prices, and reorder points. Enter dBASE IV, set the default drive and directory, and create a catalog called INVENTORY. Create the database structure and save it as PRODUCTS.

2. Modifying a Database Structure

Modify the database structure INVENTORY in Project 1, increasing the description field size and adding a Date of Reorder field. Print the database structure. Close the dBASE INVENTORY. Change to the LESSON catalog, retrieve the CARS database, and print the structure.

Editing Data

3

Imagine going to a physician's office for the first time. You fill out forms listing your name, address, employment, insurance, and medical history. The office needs this data to add to the patient database. Each question on each form is a *field*; your response is the data in the field.

You collect data in several ways. Some data you hear and trust to memory. Other data is written when you receive it, or you write the data down yourself before entering it into your computerized database. If you have determined what fields you want in your database, you know what standard information you must have to enter records in your database.

After you design your database and collect your data, you can begin to enter records. Recall that a *record* is a set of related data, such as all the items related to one patient in a medical records database. By using dBASE IV, you can store a maximum of one billion records in a database. Of course, the actual number of records you store depends on the amount of disk space available on your computer.

Adding records is only the first step in maintaining a database. You must be able to rely on the accuracy of your database information; a database is useful only if you update its contents regularly. In a patient database, the addresses, insurance providers, and places of employment change frequently. The doctor can lose time and money sending bills to the wrong address or billing an insurance carrier that no longer provides a patient coverage. dBASE IV makes updating data easy;

3

making required changes and deleting unnecessary records promptly is up to you! As you enter your first data, keep in mind that data accuracy and data security go hand in hand. No matter how carefully you update your data, you must be able to get to, or *access*, the data. Follow good documentation techniques by printing your data files periodically and backing up your data files to floppy disks or tape on a regular basis.

Objectives

1. **To Use the Browse** and Edit Screens
2. **To Add Records**
3. **To Change the Contents** of Records
4. **To Delete Records**
5. **To Use Memo Fields**

Key Terms Used in This Chapter	
Browse mode	A screen displaying up to 17 records, with fields organized horizontally across the screen.
Edit mode	A screen displaying one record with fields organized vertically down the screen.
Memo field	A type of field used to add remarks or notes within a record. The contents of a Memo field cannot exceed 64,000 characters.
Editor	The limited dBASE IV word processor. You can use the Editor to enter narrative into a Memo field.

Objective 1: To Use the Browse and Edit Screens

To help you update records, dBASE IV offers you two work surfaces where you can add and edit data. In the *Edit* work surface, you see one record at a time on-screen. In *Browse*, you see one record per line and 17 records per screen.

You can toggle between Browse mode and Edit mode by pressing [F2]. In addition, a menu bar appears above each work surface. The menu bar provides access to a series of menu options to help you add and edit data. Take a few moments to learn the general characteristics of the work surfaces and the active keys used with these work surfaces before you work with a specific database.

Accessing the Browse or Edit Work Surface

You can access the Browse or Edit work surface from the Control Center Data panel by highlighting the database you want to use and pressing [F2]. If no records have been entered into the database, the Edit work surface appears. If the database contains records, either the Edit or Browse work surface appears.

Exercise 1.1: Accessing the Browse or Edit Screen

To illustrate the data-display process, suppose that you want to edit an existing database. After you access the appropriate default disk directory and activate the catalog containing the database you want, follow these steps:

1. To access dBASE IV, select the dBASE IV option from your Custom menu or type **dbase** and then press [⏎Enter]. The Control Center appears.

2. Select the name of the database (for example, CARS) from the Data panel (see fig. 3.1).

    Press [←] or [→] to position the cursor in the Data panel; press [↓] or [↑] to position the cursor on the name of a specific database.

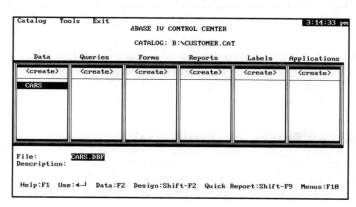

Fig. 3.1
Choosing the CARS database from the Data panel.

3 3. Press F2 to access the Browse or Edit work surface for the selected database. (Alternatively, you can press ↵Enter, select the Display Data option, and then press ↵Enter again.)

If records are already entered in the database, you see the last screen in use. You can toggle between the Browse and Edit work surfaces by pressing F2. Exit back to the Control Center by selecting Exit from the menu bar.

Understanding the Edit Work Surface

The Edit work surface displays one record at a time (see fig. 3.2). The screen displays one field of data per line and arranges the fields in one vertical column. The Edit work surface uses as many screens as are necessary to display the record. (A record structure may have as many as 255 fields.) As you scroll down (or up) the screen, some fields move off the screen, and others move on to the screen.

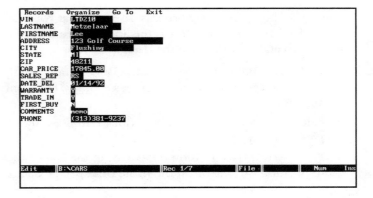

Fig. 3.2
The Edit work
surface.

Each field appears in the order that it was defined in the database structure. The field name appears first, followed by an area to enter the data. The area for entering data appears in color (or reverse video, if you have a mono-chrome monitor).

Understanding the Browse Work Surface

When you want to see and edit more than one record on-screen at a time, you can use the Browse work surface (see fig. 3.3). The screen becomes a window, panning from left to right or up to down in the database. The Browse work surface is organized into columns (fields) and rows (records). Fields appear from left to right across the screen in the order that each was defined in the database structure. Most records have too many fields to fit on one screen from left to right. Most databases have too many records to fit from the top to the bottom of a single screen; the Browse work surface can display up to 17 records per screen.

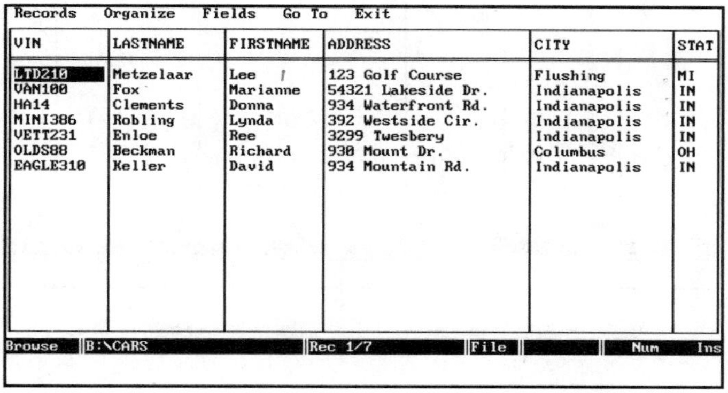

3

```
Records    Organize    Fields    Go To    Exit
VIN          LASTNAME    FIRSTNAME  ADDRESS               CITY          STAT
LTD210       Metzelaar   Lee    /   123 Golf Course       Flushing      MI
VAN100       Fox         Marianne   54321 Lakeside Dr.    Indianapolis  IN
HA14         Clements    Donna      934 Waterfront Rd.    Indianapolis  IN
MINI386      Robling     Lynda      392 Westside Cir.     Indianapolis  IN
VETT231      Enloe       Ree        3299 Tuesbery         Indianapolis  IN
OLDS88       Beckman     Richard    930 Mount Dr.         Columbus      OH
EAGLE310     Keller      David      934 Mountain Rd.      Indianapolis  IN




Browse   B:\CARS              Rec 1/7        File            Num    Ins
```

Fig. 3.3
The Browse work surface.

The structures of the Browse and Edit work surfaces—17 records in row-and-column format, or 1 record with each field below the preceding one—are built into dBASE IV. Most of your *source* documents (forms from which you collect data to enter into the database) will not match the Browse or Edit layout on-screen. Chapter 8 tells you how to create custom data-entry screens that enable you to arrange the field layout on-screen to look like the paper forms on which you collect data.

Understanding the Browse or Edit Status Bar

You may remember that the status bar displays information near the bottom of the screen, just above the navigation and message lines. The status bar information changes to describe what you are doing at the moment (see fig. 3.4).

Using Keys in Browse Mode and Edit Mode

The cursor-control keys help you move around the database and find records. You can press PgUp to move the cursor to the preceding record in Edit mode or to the preceding screenful of records in Browse mode. Many keys are active to help you navigate the Browse and Edit work surfaces. Other keys are active during certain operations, such as adding or deleting records. Take a few moments to study the lists of keystrokes that follow.

3

Fig. 3.4
The status bar.

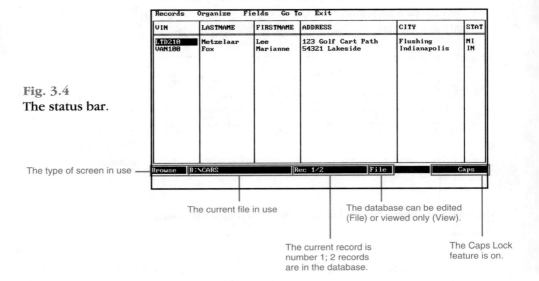

The type of screen in use ——

The current file in use

The database can be edited (File) or viewed only (View).

The current record is number 1; 2 records are in the database.

The Caps Lock feature is on.

Keys Used To Navigate in Browse Mode and Edit Mode

↑ or ↓	Moves the cursor up or down
← or →	Moves the cursor left or right
PgUp or PgDn	Moves the cursor up or down one record in Edit mode or one screenful in Browse mode
Home	Moves the cursor to the first character in the current field in Edit mode or the first field in Browse mode
End	Moves the cursor to the last character in the current field in Edit mode or the last field in Browse mode
⇧Shift + Tab↹ or F3	Moves the cursor to the previous field
Tab↹ or F4	Moves the cursor to the next field

Keys Used To Add Data in Browse Mode and Edit Mode

[Ins]	Causes existing text to shift right one character for each new character typed
[⇧Shift]+[F4]	Copies data from a field in the preceding record to the same field in the current record
[↵Enter]	Ends the entry to a field and moves the cursor to the next field

3

Keys Used To Delete Data in Browse Mode and Edit Mode

[←Backspace]	Removes the character to the left of the cursor
[Del]	Deletes the character at the cursor
[Ctrl]+[Y]	Deletes all characters to the right of the cursor
[Ctrl]+[U]	Marks a record for deletion

Other Browse and Edit Keys

[Esc]	Leaves the current record without saving changes to the current record
[F2]	Switches between Browse mode and Edit mode
[F10]	Accesses menu options

Use the keys described to edit the contents of existing records or add new records.

Objective 2: To Add Records

You can begin to enter records into a database after you create and save the database structure. You can enter your records in the Browse mode or the Edit mode. If the database has no records entered, you see an initial blank record in Edit mode. You then can begin to enter data.

If your database already contains records, you can add new records in two ways:

- You can select Records from the Browse or Edit menu bar and then select Add New Records from the Records menu.

61

- In Browse mode or Edit mode, you can press ⬇ when the current record is the last record. In Edit mode, pressing (PgDn) serves the same purpose. The following prompt appears at the bottom of the screen:

  ===> Add new records? (Y/N)

  Press (Y) to add new records.

3

Generally, you use the second method only if the current record is near the end of the file. Otherwise, use the Records menu and its Add New Records option.

When you finish entering records, be sure to quit the screen in a manner that saves your work. Do not turn off the computer without first exiting your current dBASE operation, or you risk losing data. Select Exit from the Browse menu or Edit menu and then select Exit.

When adding a large number of records, you should exit and save the database periodically and then reenter Browse mode or Edit mode to continue adding records. Saving periodically reduces the likelihood of losing work due to a power failure.

Learning the Guidelines for Entering Data into Fields

To enter data, position the cursor in the appropriate data field on a Browse or Edit work surface and then type the field's contents. Be sure to keep in mind these points:

- The cursor moves automatically to the next field if the data you enter fills the current field. A beep sounds when the field is filled, and the cursor moves to the next field.

  Typing a month-day-year combination in a date field or a **Y** (Yes) or **N** (No) in a Logical field fills the field. Typing **Indianapolis** in a City field defined as having 12 characters fills the field.

- To move to the next field if you have not filled the current field, you must press (⏎Enter).

  When you type a 12-character city name in a field defined as having 18 characters, for example, you have not filled the field.

- To move the cursor within a field, press (⬅) or (➡). If the cursor is at the beginning of a field when you press (⬅), the cursor moves to the preceding field; if the cursor is at the end of a field when you press (➡), the cursor moves to the next field.

- Press (Tab⇥) or (F4) to move the cursor to the next field. Press (⇧Shift)+(Tab⇥) or (F3) to move the cursor to the preceding field.

- Do not enter slashes (/) in a Date field (dBASE does it for you). Do not enter any punctuation (a dollar ($) sign or comma, for example) in a Numeric or Float field, except the decimal point.

- Enter data in a Memo field with the Text Editor (see the "To Use Memo Fields" section later in this chapter).

Adding Records

You can use the Edit or Browse screen to add records. Remember that in Edit mode you enter data one field after another down a column. Each field appears on the left. You type the data to the right of the field. You can press ⏎Enter or Tab⇥ to move to the next field.

Exercise 2.1: Adding Records from the Edit Screen

Follow these steps to add records in Edit mode:

1. Access the Control Center Data panel, select the database (for example, CARS), and press F2 to access the Browse or Edit screen.

   If no records have been entered in the database, skip to step 5 (a blank record in Edit mode appears automatically).

2. If the screen displays a row-and-column multiple-record Browse format, press F2 to switch to the Edit screen's columnar one-record display.

3. Press Alt + R to access the Records pull-down menu (see fig. 3.5).

   Use the Records menu to undo changes, add records, mark records for deletion, and keep the record contents blank.

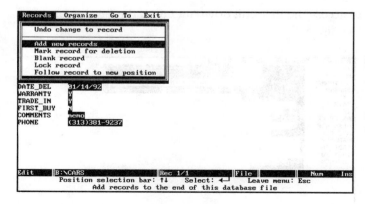

Fig. 3.5
The Records pull-down menu.

63

3

4. Press A to select Add New Records and position the cursor on the first field of a blank record.

5. Begin typing your data in the first field (see fig. 3.6).

   If you make a mistake, press ⟨◆Backspace⟩ and edit your error.

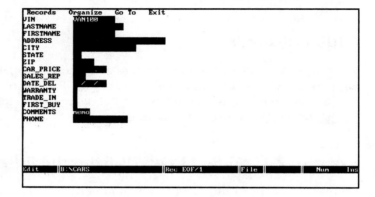

Fig. 3.6
Entering data in
the first field.

6. After you finish entering the field's contents, press ⟨↵Enter⟩ to move the cursor to the next field. (dBASE IV beeps and moves the cursor to the next field if typed contents fill a field.)

7. Continue entering data in the remaining fields of the current record. (Refer to fig. 3.8.)

   Press ⟨Tab ⇄⟩ or ⟨↵Enter⟩ to skip fields in which you do not want to enter data.

   When you have completed or bypassed all fields, dBASE IV moves to a new blank record.

8. Continue entering data in additional records.

9. Press ⟨Alt⟩+⟨E⟩ to access the Exit pull-down menu on the Browse or Edit menu bar (see fig. 3.7).

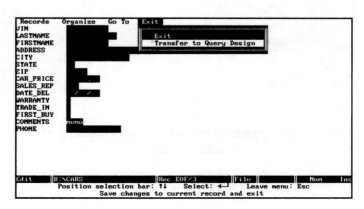

Fig. 3.7
The Exit pull-
down menu.

10. Select Exit from the Exit pull-down menu to save your changes and restore the Control Center.

Exercise 2.2: Adding Records from the Browse Screen

Browse mode (one record per row, multiple records per screen) is available after records are entered in a database. Follow these steps to add records in Browse mode:

1. Access the Control Center Data panel, select the database name, and then press F2 to access the Browse or Edit screen.

2. If the screen displays a columnar one-record Edit format, press F2 to switch to the Browse screen's row-and-column multiple-record display.

3. Press Alt + R to access the Records pull-down menu.

4. Select Add New Records to move the cursor to a blank record.

5. Enter the following data in the appropriate fields for each record.

    MXD33, James Michael, 42 Brown Ave, Long Island, NY

    JETTA21, Jill Lehigh, 201 Proctor Road, San Francisco, CA

    Enter data for each field in Browse mode, following the same guidelines you used to enter data in the Edit mode.

6. After you enter the new records, press Alt + E to access the Exit option from the menu bar. Then select Exit to save the additions and restore the Control Center.

Objective 3: To Change the Contents of Records

Just entering data is not enough to maintain your database. You must keep its contents current. The information you retrieve from your database is only as good as the data you enter. Some outdated information is inconsequential—if you reach a wrong phone number, you generally get a new listing quickly and can repeat the call. Other outdated information can be more costly—misstating a customer's balance because you fail to record a payment or distributing advertising brochures to wrong addresses, for example. Keeping data current means constantly adding records, changing data in existing records, and deleting unwanted records.

Entering changes in a dBASE IV computer-managed database is much easier than in a manual, paper-based system. Imagine working in a personnel department that maintains employee information on paper, with each employee's record in a folder stored in a file cabinet. If an employee changes name, salary level, or position, you must erase or cross out the old data and then type the new data, or you must add a revised form to the folder.

If you change the wrong item, you cannot undo the error without more erasing and retyping. A file folder can sit on a desk for hours waiting for an update and be inaccessible to other users. By contrast, a record change takes just seconds in a computer-managed system, and the updated information is immediately available to display on-screen or print. As an added feature in dBASE IV, you can undo a change and restore the original data.

Changing records in dBASE IV is as easy as adding records. As you become an experienced user, you can update your database in several creative ways, including changing many records in a single operation. For the moment, limit your changes to one record at a time.

Making Changes to One Record

To make changes to existing records, access the Browse mode or Edit mode, and follow a process similar to editing fields while adding records.

You can access the Browse and Edit work surfaces from the Control Center Data panel in one of two ways:

- Highlight the database to use and press F2 (Data).
- Highlight the database name in the Data panel, press ↵Enter, and then select Display Data from the menu.

Exercise 3.1: Editing Records in the Database

After you access the database you want, follow these steps to edit records:

1. Press F2 until your option of Edit (one record per screen) or Browse (17 records per screen) mode appears.
2. Press ↑, ↓, PgUp, or PgDn to locate the record to be changed. In this example, move the cursor to the second record.
3. Press ←, →, Tab↹, and ⇧Shift+Tab↹ to select the field to be changed. For this exercise, select the ADDRESS field (see fig 3.8). Press Ins and Del as necessary to edit the field contents.

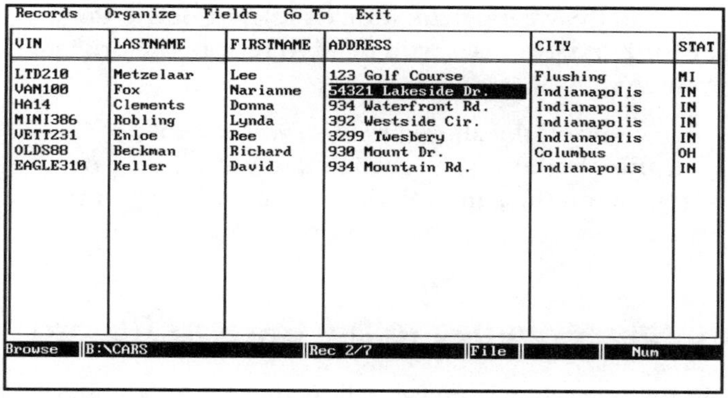

```
 Records   Organize   Fields   Go To   Exit
 VIN        LASTNAME     FIRSTNAME   ADDRESS              CITY          STAT

 LTD210     Metzelaar    Lee         123 Golf Course      Flushing      MI
 VAN100     Fox          Marianne    54321 Lakeside Dr.   Indianapolis  IN
 HA14       Clements     Donna       934 Waterfront Rd.   Indianapolis  IN
 MINI386    Robling      Lynda       392 Westside Cir.    Indianapolis  IN
 VETT231    Enloe        Ree         3299 Twesbery        Indianapolis  IN
 OLDS88     Beckman      Richard     930 Mount Dr.        Columbus      OH
 EAGLE310   Keller       David       934 Mountain Rd.     Indianapolis  IN




 Browse    B:\CARS              Rec 2/7         File         Num
```

Fig. 3.8
Selecting the
Address field.

4. Type the change into the field (see fig. 3.9).

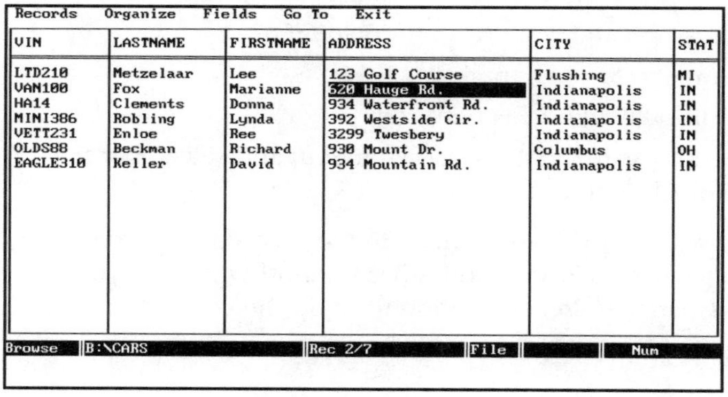

```
 Records   Organize   Fields   Go To   Exit
 VIN        LASTNAME     FIRSTNAME   ADDRESS              CITY          STAT

 LTD210     Metzelaar    Lee         123 Golf Course      Flushing      MI
 VAN100     Fox          Marianne    520 Hauge Rd.        Indianapolis  IN
 HA14       Clements     Donna       934 Waterfront Rd.   Indianapolis  IN
 MINI386    Robling      Lynda       392 Westside Cir.    Indianapolis  IN
 VETT231    Enloe        Ree         3299 Twesbery        Indianapolis  IN
 OLDS88     Beckman      Richard     930 Mount Dr.        Columbus      OH
 EAGLE310   Keller       David       934 Mountain Rd.     Indianapolis  IN




 Browse    B:\CARS              Rec 2/7         File         Num
```

Fig. 3.9
The changed
Address field.

You can save your revised record in two ways:

• You can move the cursor from the changed record to the preceding record or the next record.

• You can select Exit from the Browse or Edit menu bar. If you must locate just a few records throughout a large database, dBASE IV offers simple searches to help you find the records you need quickly.

Undoing Changes to One Record

dBASE IV offers the capability of undoing the changes just made to the current record. This feature is helpful if you make an error while you are updating a

3

record. You may revise data in the wrong field, for example, or delete the contents of the wrong record. In both cases, you need to restore the original contents of the field or record.

Caution: If you move the cursor off the altered record, you cannot use the Undo Change to Record feature because your changes are saved in the database. Instead, you must reposition the cursor in the record and retype the changes.

Exercise 3.2: Undoing a Change to the Current Record

If you made a mistake in the preceding exercise, follow these steps to undo the error made to the current record:

1. Do not move the cursor away from the current altered record (although you may move to other fields in the record).
2. Press Alt + R to access the Records pull-down menu.
3. Select Undo Change to Record option.
4. Proceed with additional editing as required.
5. Press Alt + E to access the Exit pull-down menu, and select Exit to return to the Control Center.

Remember that Undo works only if you remain in the record after making the initial change. If you make a correction and move to another record, you cannot use the Undo Change to Record option to undo the correction.

Objective 4: To Delete Records

In dBASE IV, you can delete records and still maintain them in the database. The program recognizes that you may need to keep track of out-of-date records even after you move them from your working database. Suppose that you manage a physician's patient database. You can designate all patients not seen in two years as inactive and remove those patients' records from the screen display but not from the database itself. dBASE enables you to mark records for deletion and then hide them from view. You then can unmark a record marked for deletion if a patient returns after a long absence.

As an alternative, you can mark records for deletion and then actually remove them, not hide them, from the database. The two ways of moving records from the active database have advantages and disadvantages.

If you mark and hide records, you can unmark and use them later. These hidden records, however, remain in the file and take up space. Any searches run slower because dBASE IV still must read the records before ignoring them. To help you decide how you want to handle records to remove, consider the disk space available, the speed of your disk drive and processor, and the potential size of your database if you hide deleted records.

As yet another alternative, you can avoid the speed and space problems of hiding files by copying the records you want to hide to another database on the hard disk or to a floppy disk. After safely copying the records, you can delete the original records. You then have a separate database of inactive records that you can access whenever you want.

Marking Records To Be Deleted

You must mark records before you can remove them from the database or hide them. You can mark records from the Browse or the Edit screen. Because Browse displays several records, you may decide to work from the Browse screen if you have several records to mark.

Exercise 4.1: Marking Records for Deletion

To mark a record for deletion from the Browse screen, follow these steps:

1. Open the appropriate database by highlighting the database name on the Control Data panel and pressing F2.

2. Press F2 until the Browse screen appears.

3. Press ↓ or ↑ to position the cursor on the last record.

4. Press Ctrl + U to mark the record for deletion. (Alternatively, you can press Alt + R to access the Records menu and then press M to select Mark Record for Deletion.)

   Del appears in the status bar to indicate that the record is marked (see fig. 3.10).

5. Press Alt + E to access the Exit pull-down menu, and then select Exit to return to the Control Center.

After you mark the records for deletion, you can hide them or remove them from the file.

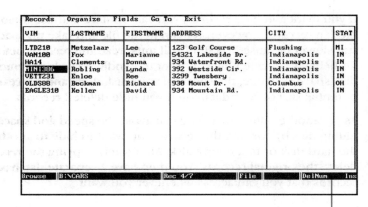

Fig. 3.10
Marking a record.

Del indicates that a record is marked.

Unmarking Records Marked for Deletion

You mark records for two reasons: to indicate records to be permanently removed from the database or to indicate records to be omitted from printed reports and screen displays.

Exercise 4.2: Unmarking Records

You can remove deletion marks by following these steps:

1. Select the database containing the records marked for deletion, and then access the Browse mode or Edit mode.

2. Press Alt + O to access the Organize pull-down menu.

3. Select Unmark All Records. The following message requesting verification appears:

    Are you sure you want to unmark all records marked
    for deletion?

4. Select No.

5. Press Alt + E to access the Exit pull-down menu, and then select Exit to return to the Control Center.

Hiding Records To Be Deleted

If you want to ignore some records in reports and searches, you can mark the records for deletion and hide them. dBASE enables you to remove marked records from view but retain them in the database.

dBASE IV uses switches, called *Set commands*, to alter its operating environment. One switch, Deleted On/Off, is normally Off. The Off setting for the switch enables you to access all records, including marked records. If you change the setting to On, you cannot access marked records, even in Browse mode or Edit mode.

Exercise 4.3: Hiding Records Marked for Deletion

To hide records previously marked for deletion, you must return to the Control Center and change the dBASE IV Deleted setting. Follow these steps:

1. Access the Control Center.
2. Press Alt + T to access the Tools pull-down menu.
3. Select the Settings option.
4. Press ↓ or ↑ to highlight the Deleted option.
5. Press ↵Enter until the word On appears next to the Deleted option (see fig. 3.11).

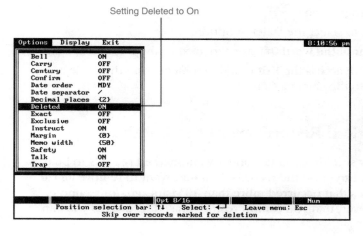

Setting Deleted to On

Fig. 3.11
Setting the Deleted option to On to hide all marked records.

6. Press [Alt]+[E] to access the Exit pull-down menu, and then select Exit to return to the Control Center.

7. Press [F2] to restore the Browse or Edit screen.

The marked record no longer appears on-screen, although the status line shows that the deleted record is still in the database.

3

Assume that you marked record 2 for deletion and set Deleted to On. If you move the cursor to record 1 and press [↓], the next record is record 3. Record 2, for all practical purposes, no longer exists.

Restoring Hidden Records

Hiding marked records removes the records from view on-screen and from reports or searches. You must unhide marked records before you try to remove them from the database.

Exercise 4.4: Revealing Hidden Records

You can restore hidden records to view if you set the Deleted option to Off. Follow these steps:

1. Access the Control Center.

2. Press [Alt]+[T] to access the Tools pull-down menu.

3. Select the Settings option.

4. Press [↓] or [↑] to select the Deleted option.

5. Press [↵Enter] until the word Off appears next to the Deleted option.

6. Press [Alt]+[E] to access the Exit pull-down menu, and then select Exit to return to the Control Center.

Removing Marked Records from the Database

If you are absolutely sure that you no longer want marked records to be part of the database, you can erase the records. You may want to remove all car sales records for sales that occurred more than 10 years ago, for example. Keep in mind, however, that you cannot restore erased records as you can hidden records.

Exercise 4.5: Removing Marked Records

To remove the record marked for deletion and view remaining records, follow these steps:

1. Select the database containing the record marked for deletion and then access Browse mode or Edit mode.

2. Press Alt+O to access the Organize pull-down menu (see fig. 3.12).

    The last two options on the Organize menu relate to the record marked for deletion.

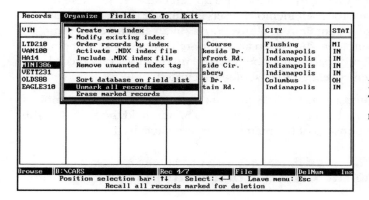

Fig. 3.12
The Organize menu.

3. Select Erase Marked Records.

    A message appears, asking you to confirm that you want to erase all marked records.

    If you select Yes, the marked record will be deleted. If you select No, the marked record remain in the file. For safety reasons, No is the default.

4. Respond to the message by selecting Yes.

5. Press Alt+E to access the Exit pull-down menu, and then select Exit to return to the Control Center.

6. Press F2 to restore the Browse mode or Edit mode, and then press F2 until the Browse screen appears.

The record marked for deletion is no longer in the database, and the record count has been adjusted from seven to six.

Unlike hidden records, erased records are no longer in the database and cannot be retrieved. Remaining records in the database are renumbered.

Objective 5: To Use Memo Fields

dBASE IV Memo fields are unique types of data that deserve special discussion. A Memo field in a database structure appears to have a 10-character width. dBASE IV uses the field, however, to locate a document associated with each record. Each document can hold up to 64,000 characters. A database structure can contain any number of Memo fields. An employee database may contain one Memo field for documenting excessive absenteeism and another Memo field for performance-appraisal data, for example.

Using a Memo field rather than a Character field can conserve valuable disk storage because space for each memo is reserved outside the database. Many employee records may contain few, if any, entries in an absenteeism comments field, for example. If you set up absenteeism comments as a Character field, not a Memo field, space would be reserved on disk for every record whether or not an entry related to absenteeism existed.

As a general rule, choose Character as the data type if the contents will not exceed 256 characters. If you do choose to use a Memo field, be sure that you understand the relationship of the memo file to the database file.

Understanding the Concept of a Memo Field

A Memo field doesn't actually contain data. Each Memo field points to a memo file in which the data is stored. The memo file has the same name as the database but has the extension DBT. If you see a lowercase memo in the database structure screen, the Memo field does not contain data. If you see an uppercase MEMO, the Memo field does contain data. When you copy the database file, do not forget to copy the memo file, too.

Entering and Editing Data in a Memo Field

dBASE IV provides an Editor work surface on which to enter data in Memo fields. The Editor functions much like a word processing program.

To enter data into Memo fields, type text in Insert or Typeover mode. The typed text word wraps to fit within the present margins. Press ⏎Enter to end a paragraph or to add space between paragraphs. Press →, ←, ↑, or ↓ to scroll through text. Press Tab⇥ to indent paragraphs.

The Editor also enables you to move, copy, and delete blocks of text; to search and replace data; and to write or read data to or from an ASCII text file.

Exercise 5.1: Entering Data in Memo Fields

To enter or edit data in a Memo field, follow these steps:

1. Select the appropriate database in the Control Center Data panel and then press [F2] to access the Browse mode or Edit mode.

2. Press [Tab⇥] or [⇧Shift]+[Tab⇥] to position the cursor in the Memo field to be edited.

3. Press [F9], and the editing screen appears.

4. Enter the text shown in figure 3.13 in the Editor work surface.

   Use Insert or Typeover mode to make corrections or add data as necessary.

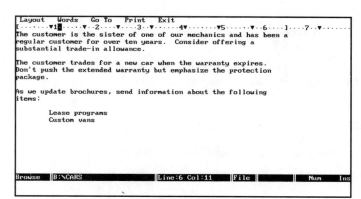

Fig. 3.13
Entering text in the Editor work surface.

5. Press [Alt]+[E] to access the Exit option from the Editor menu bar.

6. Select Save Changes and Exit or select Abandon Changes and Exit.

If you choose to abandon the Editor screen, you see the additional prompt:

    Are you sure you want to abandon operation?

Select Yes or No. You can view your finished memo on-screen or you can print it.

Chapter Summary

This chapter explained techniques to add, edit, and delete records in a dBASE IV database. You now have a database with records that can be manipulated. Chapter 4 introduces sorting and selecting records in a database.

Testing Your Knowledge

True/False Questions

1. You can toggle between Browse mode and Edit mode by pressing F2.

2. Each field in Edit mode appears in alphabetical order.

3. Pressing Ins causes existing text to shift right one character for each new character typed.

4. You can begin to enter records into a database after you create and save the database structure.

5. If you make a correction and move to another record, you can undo the correction by choosing Undo Change to Record.

Multiple Choice Questions

1. You can toggle between the Browse and Edit screens by pressing

   A. PgUp

   B. F2

   C. Tab ⇆

   D. →

   E. ⇧Shift + F2

2. Pressing Esc from the Browse and Edit screens

   A. switches between Browse mode and Edit mode.

   B. accesses menu options.

   C. leaves the current record without saving changes to the current record.

   D. marks a record for deletion.

   E. displays an error box.

3. Pressing F2, pressing Alt + R, and selecting Add New Records

    A. displays a blank line in Browse mode or a blank record in the vertical display.

    B. displays the last record entered.

    C. places the cursor at the beginning of the database.

    D. copies the last record to a new position.

    E. displays a prompt to add records.

4. In order to delete a record, you must

    A. be in the Database Structure screen.

    B. be in Browse mode.

    C. mark the record for deletion in Browse mode by pressing Ctrl + U and then remove it from the file.

    D. mark it for deletion.

    E. mark, hide, and remove the record.

5. If your Memo field contains data, you see

    A. Memo in the field.

    B. memo in the field.

    C. MEMO in the field.

    D. data in the field.

    E. MEMO in the record.

Fill-in-the-Blank Questions

1. If no records have been entered in the database, the _____ work surface appears.

2. Use the _____ work surface when you want to _____ and _____ more than one record on-screen at a time.

3. To mark a record for deletion, press _____.

4. Hidden marked records are removed from _____ but are retained in the _____.

5. A _____ field in a database structure appears to have a 10-character width.

Review: Short Projects

1. Adding Records to the SAMPLE Database

   Select the database SAMPLE, and add the following fields:

   > Address with width 20
   >
   > City with width 10
   >
   > State with width 2
   >
   > ZIP code with width 5

   Make up data for five records and add the records to the database. Save the database as SAMPLE2.

2. Adding Student Records

   Choose the CLASS catalog, make up data for five records and add the records to the STUDENT database, and then print a Quick report. Save it as STUDENT.

3. Using Memo Type and Marking Records

   Select the STUDENT database, add a field called Comment, and set it up as a Memo type. Delete the first record of the database. Mark the record and remove it. Type a Memo field for the remaining records, and save your work as STUDENT2.

Review: Long Projects

1. Adding to a Database

   Select the catalog INVENTORY, and modify the structure of the PRODUCT database. Add a field called Note, and use the Memo data type. Make up five products and add them to the database, including a memo to note the availability of the product. Print the database using the Quick Report feature. Save your work as PRODUCTS.

2. Creating a New Database

   Be sure that you are in the INVENTORY catalog. Create a new database, called EQUIPMENT, to track the model number, type of equipment, age of the equipment, date of purchase, and purchase price. Make up data for five pieces of equipment, and add the data to the database. Save the database as EQUIPMENT.

3

Organizing Data

4

Y ou have created several databases in the previous chapters. Now suppose that you want to find certain data within each database. Remember that in manual record-keeping you would have to look through the files until you found the data you needed. If you maintain your database electronically on dBASE IV, however, you can rearrange records according to the contents of any field so that you can find the records you need. You can order records by last names, for example, and quickly change to a record arrangement based on dates or types of data.

In this chapter you learn the variety of ways to organize your database records for output to screen or printer and for ease of editing multiple records.

Objectives

1. To Organize Records in dBASE IV
2. To Organize Data with an Index
3. To Create a Multiple-Key Index
4. To Create an Index That Is Not Case-Sensitive
5. To Select, Modify, and Remove an Index
6. To Edit a Database with an Index in Control

Key Terms Used in This Chapter	
Sort	The process of physically organizing each database record on disk according to the contents of a selected field (record key).
Index	The process of organizing each record by pointing to a tag for every record in the database.
Tags	Items (sometimes called index records) that contain only the record key and instructions about the location of the complete record. Records are not physically rearranged when organized by an index.
Record key	A field on which to organize records. You can use the LAST_NAME field in a membership database as the record key, for example, to organize records by members' last names.
Collating sequence	A built-in set of rules that dictates the sequence in which records are sorted or indexed. The usual order places field contents beginning with blanks first; field contents beginning with special characters second; and then field contents beginning with numbers, then uppercase letters, and finally lowercase letters.

Objective 1: To Organize Records in dBASE IV

You can rearrange your database on any field or combination of fields you want. You first should understand the terms *record keys* and *collating sequence*. Then you can decide whether to rearrange records by using an index operation or a sort operation.

Using Record Keys

Before you decide how to organize your records, you must select useful record keys. In database terminology, the field on which your database records are organized is the *record key*. All files have one or more data items suitable for use as a record key. Figure 4.1 shows an example in which the records are organized by last name.

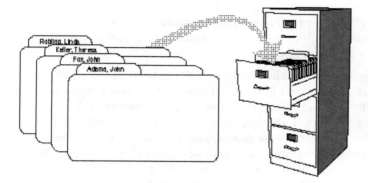

Fig. 4.1
The last name used as the record key.

Record keys can change. You might want to organize and access employee records in order of employee name, department, or date of hire, for example. In figure 4.2, the records are organized by Social Security number.

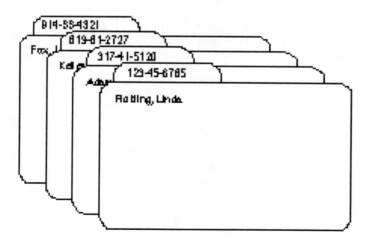

Fig. 4.2
The Social Security number field used as the record key.

In a manual file, you can have only one record key. To change the record key, you must rearrange the records or create a second copy of all records and then file the copies in a different order. Using a computerized database, you can establish multiple record keys, rearranging records according to the contents of any field.

Understanding the Collating Sequence

4

After you pick the record key or keys on which to organize your records, your computer operates with a built-in set of rules—rules that dictate the order of records after a sort or an index operation.

Suppose that you organize the records in an inventory database according to the part number field. Assume that one record does not contain a part number (the field is blank), another record contains the part number B025, another record contains the part number 7803, and another record contains the part number a456. The records are rearranged according to rules that state whether blank fields should appear first or last, whether fields starting with numbers should precede or follow fields starting with alphabetic characters, and whether fields starting with uppercase letters should precede or follow those starting with lowercase letters.

The rules determine the collating sequence. The usual collating sequence places blank fields first and special characters next, followed by numbers, uppercase letters, and lowercase letters.

dBASE IV offers four alternative collating sequences for arranging your data. Notice how each of the four options sorts the same list of names.

	Order	*Example*
Ascending	A...Z	ALBERT
ASCII	a...z	BOB
	0...9	Bob
		albert
Descending	z...a	albert
ASCII	Z...A	Bob
	9...0	BOB
		ALBERT

	Order	Example
Ascending	Aa...Zz	ALBERT
Dictionary	0...9	albert
		BOB
		Bob
Descending	zZ...aA	Bob
Dictionary	9...0	BOB
		albert
		ALBERT

4

Record keys indicate *what* to organize. In terms of *how* to organize, dBASE offers two choices: sorting and indexing. Both methods have the same result of arranging the database in a sequence that makes sense to you, but each method works differently. After you determine record keys and understand the rules for rearranging letters or numbers (collating sequence), you can decide whether you want to index or sort your records.

Indexing Records

Indexing records is generally preferred over sorting. Very simply, database records organized with an index are not physically sorted. The original database remains intact, and dBASE creates a user-specified index within a separate file called a *master index*. Each separate index contains only the record key—just a small part of the whole record—and instructions (or *pointers*) to locate each whole record.

	Database Index Created on Last Name		
Record	*LAST_NAME Field*	*Record Key*	*Pointer*
1	Robling	Adams	2
2	Adams	Fox	4
3	Keller	Keller	3
4	Fox	Robling	1

The database has several fields, including a LAST_NAME field. Records appear in the order in which they were entered. The index record contains only the record key (LAST_NAME field) and a pointer to the location of the complete record.

One advantage of an index is the speed with which records are accessed. An index accesses records quickly because the contents are very small records. An index operation does not need to read each large record into dBASE IV one character at a time. Instead, dBASE reads each shorter record key in the index, which is already in the record key sequence, and then displays or prints the actual records in the order of the record keys in the index. Although the printed copy is organized by last name, the database is not stored in order by last name.

4

Sorting Records

Sorting involves physically arranging each record according to a selected record key and placing the results in a separate file. One advantage to a sort is that you can have several keys, mixing data types as well as ascending and descending options, to form a sort key. You might sort initially on the date of a car sale in descending order (most recent date first), for example, and within each date further sort records on the last name of the car buyer in ascending order. Mixing the Date field type and Character field type is fairly easy in a dBASE IV sort operation. (The same combination in an index operation would require converting Date data to Character data before rearranging records.)

Several major disadvantages of sorting generally outweigh advantages. Sorting a file requires more time than indexing a file because entire records must be moved, often several times, before the sort is complete. The results of a sort are placed in a separate file, thus requiring much more disk space than an index.

Exercise 1.1: Sorting a File

To sort a file, follow these steps:

1. Access the Control Center screen, set the appropriate disk drive directory and catalog, and then highlight the name of the database, CARS in this case.

2. Press F2 to access the Browse work surface. (If the Edit work surface appears, press F2 again.)

3. Press Alt + O to access the Organize pull-down menu.

4. Select Sort Database on Field List.

   The cursor is in the Field Order column, ready for you to enter the first sort key.

5. Press ⌐Shift⌐ + ⌐F1⌐ to access the picklist of field names, as shown in figure 4.3.

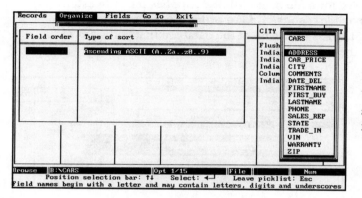

Fig. 4.3
Use the picklist to select a sort key field.

6. Highlight the name of the initial field on which to sort and press ⌐Enter⌐. For this exercise, choose LASTNAME. The field name is transferred to the Field Order column (see fig. 4.4).

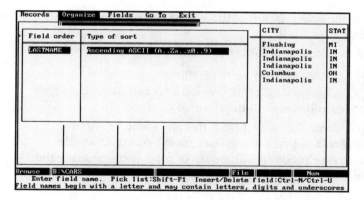

Fig. 4.4
LASTNAME is transferred to the Field Order column.

7. Press ⌐Tab⌐ to move the cursor to the Type of Sort column.

8. Press the space bar until Ascending Dictionary (Aa..Zz 0..9) appears and then press ⌐Enter⌐.

The sort key is complete. If you wanted to add another sort key, you would move the cursor down to the next line and repeat steps 4 through 7.

9. Press ⬇ until the cursor is on a blank line, and then press ↵Enter to exit the sort process.

10. Enter your choice for a file name (dBASE supplies the DBF extension) at the Enter name of sorted file prompt (see fig. 4.5). In this example, CARSLAST is the name of the database that you want to create to hold the sorted data.

4

Fig. 4.5
The prompt to
enter the name of
the database that
will hold the
sorted data.

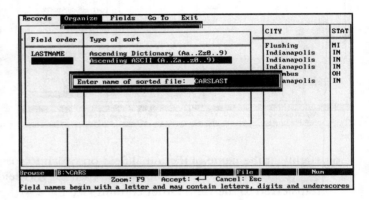

11. If you want to enter a description of the sorted file, respond to the following prompt:

    Edit the description of this .dbf file

    Otherwise, press ↵Enter to bypass the prompt.

12. Press Alt+E to access the Exit pull-down menu and then select Exit to save the changes and return to the Control Center.

Upon returning to the Control Center, notice that the name of the new database created in the sort appears in the Data panel. You can view the sorted results in the Browse mode or Edit mode or print them by using the Quick Report feature discussed in Chapter 1.

To view the new database, highlight CARSLAST as the database file. You then can see the records physically rearranged in order of last name.

Objective 2: To Organize Data with an Index

Using indexes to organize your data is simple. Create as many indexes as you need, either at the time you create the database structure or later, using the

Organize menu. Forget about the indexes until you need to rearrange your database records for display on-screen or for printing and then tell dBASE IV to activate a specific index.

Only the index that controls your file can be active at a time. You can have up to 47 indexes open (available) at one time, however. Although only one index controls the data organization, all indexes are updated when you add, change, or delete records.

If you choose to rearrange records by using an index, dBASE keeps the original order of records in the database file with the DBF extension and creates a master index file with the same name but with an MDX extension.

4

Exercise 2.1: Creating a Database and Adding Records

To create a database and then add records, follow these steps:

1. Access the catalog Lessons and create the database MEMBERS, as shown in figure 4.6. Be sure to designate the Index fields with Y or N as shown.

2. Add the records displayed in figure 4.7. Use Chapter 2 as a reference.

Num	Field Name	Field Type	Width	Dec	Index
1	BILL_LNAME	Character	20		Y
2	BILL_FNAME	Character	15		Y
3	MEM_DATE	Date	8		N
4	MEM_TYPE	Character	1		Y
5	DUES	Numeric	5	0	N
6	DUES_DUE	Numeric	2	0	N
7	SIG	Character	12		Y

Bytes remaining: 3937

Database C:\dbsample\<NEW>   Field 7/7   Num
Enter the field name. Insert/Delete field:Ctrl-N/Ctrl-U
Field names begin with a letter and may contain letters, digits and underscores

Fig. 4.6
The structure of the new database, Members.

Creating an Index in the Database Structure

You can create indexes when you create or modify the database structure. Simply press Y in the Index column, and the new index is added to the master index. (Changing an entry from Y to N in the Index column removes the index from the master index.)

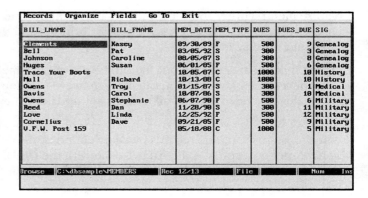

Fig. 4.7
The records
contained in the
Members database.

Exercise 2.2: Creating an Index in an Existing Database

To create an index by modifying an existing database structure, follow these steps:

1. Access the Control Center screen, set the appropriate disk drive directory and catalog, and then highlight MEMBERS, the name of the database.

2. Press ⇧Shift + F2 to access the Database Design work surface, and then press Esc.

   The Index column indicates that indexes have already been established for four fields (BILL_LNAME, BILL_FNAME, MEM_TYPE, and SIG).

3. Press ↓ and ↑ until the highlight bar rests on the name of a field you want to index. In this exercise, highlight MEM_DATE.

4. Press Tab⇄ and ⇧Shift + Tab⇄ until the cursor rests in the Index column of the chosen field.

5. Press Y to use the chosen field as an index (see fig. 4.8).

6. Press Alt + E to access the Exit pull-down menu, and then choose Exit to save the changes and return to the Control Center.

When you exit the Database Design work surface after creating an index, a window appears on-screen. This window displays information about the index being created. After a few seconds, the window disappears.

Using the Database Design work surface is the easiest way to create and delete an index. Each index created on the Design work surface, however, can contain only one field. On occasion, you need to create a single index using two or more fields. For that purpose, you need to use the Organize menu.

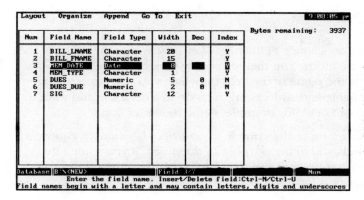

Fig. 4.8
The Index column
indicates that an
additional index
has been estab-
lished for the
MEM_DATE field.

4

Creating an Index from the Organize Menu

As an alternative to specifying an index in the database structure, you can use
the Create New Index option on the Organize menu to create a new index.

You can access the Organize menu from the Browse or Edit work surface
(dBASE IV Version 1.1 or later) or the Database Design work surface.

Exercise 2.3: Using the Organize Menu To Create an Index

Follow these steps to open the Organize pull-down menu from the Browse or
Edit work surface:

1. Access the Control Center screen, set the appropriate disk drive
   directory and catalog, and highlight the MEMBERS database.

2. Press F2 to access the Browse or Edit work surface.

3. Press Alt + O to access the Organize menu.

To open the Organize pull-down menu from the Database Design work
surface, simply press Alt + O .

The first option on the Organize pull-down menu enables you to create a
new index. You complete up to five items on the Create New Index menu to
describe the index. The first two items, Name of Index and Index Expression,
require completion. The last three items—FOR Clause, Order of Index, and
Display First Duplicate Key Only—contain defaults you can accept or change.

Naming an Index

If you set up an index on a single field (*single-key index*), use the name of the field as the name of the index. You then can easily remember the name of the index by just recalling the name of the field on which you want to rearrange records. If you have name and address information in a database and want to set an index on the State field, for example, name the index State.

If you set up an index on more than one field (*multiple-key index*), choose a field name that reminds you of the purpose of the index. If you want a list of addresses rearranged first by state and then by city within state, for example, name the index Statecity.

Follow the same conventions to name an index as you do to name a field. Index names must begin with a letter and may contain up to nine more letters, numbers, and the underscore character.

Exercise 2.4: To Enter an Index Name

Follow these steps to enter an index name:

1. Select Create new index from the Organize pull-down menu.
2. Press N to choose Name of Index (see fig. 4.9).
3. For this exercise, type the index name, INTEREST (see fig. 4.10).

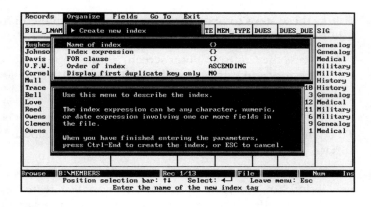

Fig. 4.9
Select Name of Index from the Create New Index menu.

4. Press ↵Enter to return to the Create New Index menu.

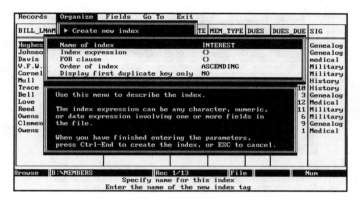

Fig. 4.10
Enter the name of
the index.

Defining an Index Expression

The Index Expression option on the Create New Index menu defines how dBASE makes the new index. That is, the expression you define tells dBASE what field or fields to use when rearranging the records. You cannot use logical and memo fields to establish an index.

If you know the rules for typing the conditions for your new index and remember the field names you want to use, start typing. Otherwise, watch the Navigation line for instructions. One feature you can use to form an index expression is the Expression Builder.

Exercise 2.5: Defining an Index Expression on a Single Field

To define an index expression on a single field, select the Create New Index option from the Organize pull-down menu and follow these steps:

1. Press ⎵ to select Index Expression.

   Note: At this point, you can type the field or field combination on which to base the rearrangement of records, and press ↵Enter. If you prefer on-screen assistance with the definition process, complete the remaining steps.

2. Following the instructions in the Navigation line, press ⇧Shift+ F1 to access the Expression Builder display, shown in figure 4.11.

91

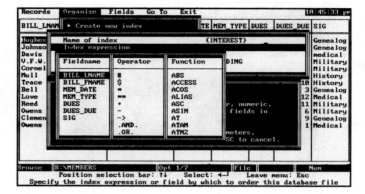

Fig. 4.11
The Expression
Builder display.

The Expression Builder display contains three columns to assist you in entering an index expression: *Fieldname* lists field names from the current database structure; *Operator* lists symbols used to join fields; and *Function* lists programmed dBASE features used to manipulate data.

3. Press ← and → until the cursor is positioned in the Fieldname column.

4. Press ↑ and ↓ until the cursor rests on the field name you want to use for an index. In this exercise, highlight the field name SIG.

5. Press ←Enter to transfer the highlighted field name to the Index Expression box.

   The new index named INTEREST organizes records based on the SIG (special interest group) field chosen from the Expression Builder display.

6. Press Ctrl + End to complete the minimum specifications—name and field definition—for an index and to return to the Create New Index menu.

When the database is under the control of an index, by default data appears in ascending order based on the contents of the field defined by the index. In this example, all membership records appear in ascending order based on special interest groups: Genealogy, History, Medical, and Military.

Specifying the Index Order

Use the Order of Index option from the Create New Index menu to specify ascending (A to Z) or descending (Z to A) order. In an ascending index, capital letters come before lowercase letters—*Drum* comes before *apple*, for example. In descending-order indexes, capital letters come after lowercase letters—*apple* appears before *Drum*. The default is ascending order, which in most situations is the correct setting.

Exercise 2.6: Changing the Index Order

To change this setting, select the Create New Index option from the Organize pull-down menu and follow these steps:

1. Press Ⓞ to select Order of Index.
2. Press the space bar to toggle between ascending and descending order of records.
3. When the setting you want to use displays, press ⏎Enter to return to the Create New Index Menu.

Displaying the First Duplicate Key Only

You can use the Display First Duplicate Key Only option from the Create new Index menu to tell dBASE IV to include only the first of multiple records sharing the same index value. Suppose that you have a file with names and addresses including a CITY field. To produce a list of all the cities in which your customers live without displaying duplicate city entries, set the Display First Duplicate Key Only option to Yes.

Exercise 2.7: Changing the First Duplicate Key Only Option

To alter this option to restrict the display of field contents to unique entries, select the Create New Index option from the Organize pull-down menu and follow these steps:

1. Press Ⓓ to select Display First Duplicate Key Only.
2. Press the space bar to toggle between the Yes and No settings. For this exercise, press the space bar until Yes appears.
3. Press ⏎Enter to return to the Create New Index menu.

When a database is under the control of an index option to display only the first duplicate key, the display of contents is limited to unique entries in the indexed field (see fig. 4.12).

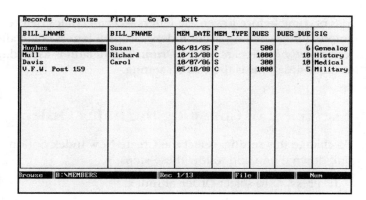

Fig. 4.12
Membership
records are limited
to the first occur-
rence of each
interest category.

Saving a New Index

You can save a new index if you have specified at least the first two options on
the Create New Index menu.

Exercise 2.8: Saving the Index

To save the index settings and exit to the Control Center, follow these steps:

1. Following screen instructions, press Ctrl + End to save the index.
   Press Esc to quit without saving the new index. The work surface
   from which you initially accessed the Organize menu reappears.

2. Select Exit from the Database Design or the Browse or Edit menu bar
   and then complete the process to exit to the Control Center.

Pressing Ctrl + End causes the new index to be placed in control of the
database automatically. When you return to the Browse or Edit work surface,
you see your records arranged according to the just-defined field or field
combination. Always check to see that any rearranged records are in the order
you want and modify the index if changes are warranted.

Objective 3: To Create a Multiple-Key Index

You have seen dBASE IV's capability of rearranging records based on one field.
Seeing hundreds of records in an address database rearranged by last name in
a matter of seconds is impressive. In addition, dBASE IV enables you to
reorder records on more than one field—a *multiple-key index*—and even
create new information in the process.

94

You can easily activate an index that reorders records based on more than one field. Think about student records kept by a college—including the data fields FIRST_NAME, LAST_NAME, MAJOR, SEX, AGE, and ENTER_DATE (enrollment date). Assume that the records in the database stored on disk are in the order in which they were entered in the database—no order. There are many useful ways to reorder the records for printing or on-screen display.

You can establish an index on MAJOR only, but think about how much more information you would have if you first arranged the records by MAJOR, then by SEX within MAJOR, and then by AGE within SEX. You can establish multiple-key indexes by joining field names with an operator, such as the plus sign (+). Specify the most important field, then the most important field within that field, and so on. The field expression for the multiple-key college example would be MAJOR+SEX+AGE.

Consider another example. Suppose that you keep an inventory database that includes the fields DESC (description), UNITPRICE, and ON_HAND (quantity on hand). You can reorder the records based on each item's total cost in descending order—yet total cost isn't even a field in the database! Just join the numeric fields UNITPRICE and ON_HAND with the multiplication operator (*) when you indicate a field expression.

Until you are quite familiar with the format of typing an index expression, use the on-screen assistance provided by the Expression Builder display, which you access from the Organize menu. Remember that the box displays a Fieldname column, an Operator column, and a Function column. To *concatenate* (put together) two or more fields to act as a single key, make selections from the Fieldname and Operator columns.

Exercise 3.1: Creating a Multiple-Key Index

Assume that you have accessed the Organize menu from the Browse or Edit work surface and are now ready to enter the specifications for a multiple-key index. Follow these steps:

1. Select Create New Index from the Organize menu.
2. Select Name of Index.
3. Type the name for the index, **INTEREST**, and then press ⏎Enter.
4. Select Index Expression.
5. Press ⇧Shift + F1 to activate the three-column Expression Builder display.
6. Select the field name **SIG** from the Fieldname column.

7. Press ⸰Shift⸏ + ⸰F1⸏ and then select an operator. For this example, select **+**.

8. Press ⸰Shift⸏ + ⸰F1⸏ and then select the second field, **BILL_LNAME**, from the Fieldname column.

   To use more fields, continue selecting all the field names and operators to comprise the index expression before you press ⸰↵Enter⸏.

   The multiple-key index shown in figure 4.13 organizes data initially by special interest group (SIG) and by last name (BILL_LNAME) within special interest group.

9. Press ⸰↵Enter⸏ to complete the index field expression.

Fig. 4.13
An example of a multiple-key index.

BILL_LNAME	BILL_FNAME	MEM_DATE	MEM_TYPE	DUES	DUES_DUE	SIG
Bell	Pat	03/05/92	S	300	3	Genealog
Clements	Kasey	09/30/89	F	500	9	Genealog
Hughes	Susan	06/01/85	F	500	6	Genealog
Johnson	Caroline	08/05/87	S	300	8	Genealog
Mull	Richard	10/13/88	C	1000	10	History
Trace Your Roots		10/05/87	C	1000	10	History
Davis	Carol	10/07/86	S	300	10	Medical
Love	Linda	12/25/92	F	500	12	Medical
Owens	Troy	01/15/87	S	300	1	Medical
Cornelius	Dave	09/21/85	F	500	9	Military
Owens	Stephanie	06/07/90	F	500	6	Military
Reed	Dan	11/20/90	S	300	11	Military
V.F.W. Post 159		05/18/88	C	1000	5	Military

Browse   B:\MEMBERS   Rec 8/13   File   NumCaps

10. When you complete all index settings, press ⸰Ctrl⸏ + ⸰End⸏ to save the index and restore the Browse or Edit work surface.

Objective 4: To Create an Index That Is Not Case-Sensitive

dBASE IV is a case-sensitive database program because it treats upper- and lowercase letters differently. This fact can be a problem if data controlled by an index contains lowercase first letters or a mixture of upper- and lowercase letters, for example. Figure 4.14 shows a situation in which a case-sensitive special interest group index controls the database. The lowercase *medical* entry appears out of alphabetic sequence, positioned after the other entries that begin with an uppercase letter.

```
 Records   Organize   Fields   Go To   Exit

 BILL_FNAME      MEM_DATE  MEM_TYPE  DUES  DUES_DUE  SIG

 Susan          06/01/85  F          500        6  Genealogy
 Caroline       08/05/87  S          300        8  Genealogy
 Pat            03/05/92  S          300        3  Genealogy
 Kasey          09/30/89  F          500        9  Genealogy
 Richard        10/13/88  C         1000       10  History
                10/05/87  C         1000       10  History
 Linda          12/25/92  F          500       12  Medical
 Troy           01/15/87  S          300        1  Medical
                05/18/88  C         1000        5  Military
 Dave           09/21/85  F          500        9  Military
 Dan            11/20/90  S          300       11  Military
 Stephanie      06/07/90  F          500        6  Military
 Carol          10/07/86  S          300       10  medical

 Browse    B:\MEMBERS              Rec 3/13        File              Num
```

Fig. 4.14
A case-sensitive
index can cause
organizational
problems.

dBASE's Expression Builder lists 130 functions with which you can manipulate
your data. Two of the functions are UPPER( ) and LOWER( ). These options
cause an index to treat upper- and lowercase characters the same. Without
changing the data in the database, UPPER( ) shifts the data in the index to
uppercase. LOWER( ) shifts data to lowercase.

Exercise 4.1: Using a Non-Case-Sensitive Index

Before you try this exercise, be sure to change the SIG field in the Davis
record to *medical* (all lowercase). Then, to see how the UPPER( ) function
causes dBASE IV to handle all letters in the indexed data as uppercase, follow
these steps:

1. Select Create New Index from the Organize menu, and then select
   Name of Index from the Create New Index menu.
2. Type the name for the index, UPPER_SIG, and then press ⏎Enter.
3. Select Index Expression.
4. Press ⇧Shift + F1 to activate the three-column Expression Builder
   display.
5. Move the cursor to the Function column, highlight UPPER, and press
   ⏎Enter.
6. Press ← to position the cursor on top of the right parenthesis in the
   index expression.
7. Press ⇧Shift + F1 and then ← and → to access the Fieldname column, and select the field name to be used with the UPPER( ) function.
8. Press ⏎Enter to complete specification of the index field expression
   (see fig. 4.15).

97

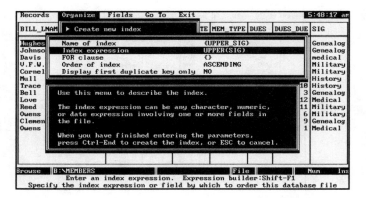

Fig. 4.15
This non-case-sensitive index organizes data by special interest group (SIG).

9. When you have completed all index settings, press ⌈Ctrl⌉+⌈End⌉ to save the index and restore the Browse or Edit work surface.

When a non-case-sensitive special interest group index controls the database, the lowercase *medical* entry appears in sequence with other mixed-case medical entries.

Objective 5: To Select, Modify, and Remove an Index

Perhaps by now you are beginning to see the importance of the creation process in database software. Analyzing what you need from your database (information) in order to understand what you need to place in the database (data) takes time. Even more time is needed to create useful indexes that control the output of information to the screen or printer in a meaningful sequence. You must know how to activate a database to add, edit, and delete records. You also must be able to activate an index and then modify or delete it as necessary.

Selecting an Index

Remember that indexes are stored in a master index file (MDX) with the same name as the database file (DBF). When you put a database into use, usually from the Control Center Data panel, all associated indexes automatically open. As you update the database by adding, altering, or deleting records, all indexes update as well—automatically. If you want to see your data in one of the indexed sequences, however, you must specify which index you want to use to control the order of the data.

Exercise 5.1: Activating an Existing Index

To activate an index previously stored in the master index file, follow these steps:

1. Access the Control Center screen, set the appropriate disk drive directory and catalog, and highlight the MEMBERS database.

2. Press F2 to access the Browse or Edit screen.

3. Press Alt+O to access the Organize menu, and select Order Records by Index (see fig. 4.16).

The list of index names in the active master index file (MDX)

The index expression for the first index in the list

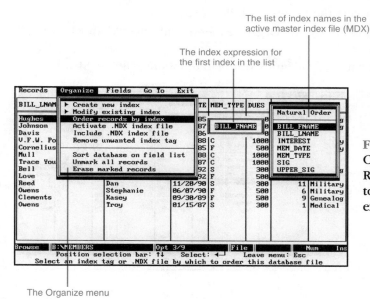

The Organize menu

Fig. 4.16
Choose Order Records by Index to activate an existing index.

4. Select the index you plan to use, INTEREST.

Be sure to activate the index you want before using the Browse mode or Edit mode and then printing reports or labels. The just-activated index remains in control until you activate a different index or close the file at the Control Center Data panel.

Modifying an Index

If an index already exists, use the Organize menu's Modify Existing Index option to change the index criteria. The option functions exactly like the Create New Index option—with one difference. When you select the index to be modified, you can see current specifications in the fields. You must specify at least the first two of four index criteria: the name of the index and one or more fields on which to index.

Exercise 5.2: Modifying an Existing Index

To modify an index, follow these steps:

1. Access the Control Center screen, set the appropriate disk drive directory and catalog, and highlight the MEMBERS database.

2. Press F2 to access the Browse or Edit screen.

3. Press Alt + O to access the Organize menu, and select Modify Existing Index (see fig. 4.17).

4. Highlight the name of the index you plan to modify, UPPER_SIG.

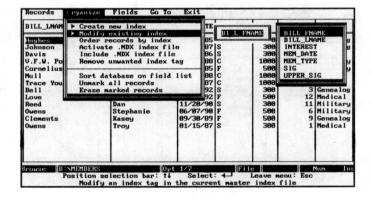

Fig. 4.17
The pop-up list of
existing indexes
appears.

5. Press ↵Enter to display the Index Expression menu.

6. Modify the expression by typing or using the Expression Builder feature. In this example, select Index Expression, press ↵Enter, and then type in a new expression (use the UPPER( ) function with the BILL_LNAME field).

7. Press Ctrl + End to save your changes and exit to the Organize menu, or press Esc to exit without saving your changes.

Removing an Index

As you examine your database structures, you may find an index that you no longer use. Because any index takes up space on disk and affects the speed of dBASE IV in Browse mode or Edit mode, remove from disk any indexes that you are not using regularly. Remember that you can easily create the index again if you need it. The more records your database contains, the more your database speed is affected by the number of indexes in use.

Exercise 5.3: Removing an Index Tag

To remove an index tag from the master index, follow these steps:

1. Select the MEMBERS database, and then access the Browse mode or Edit mode or Database Design work surface.
2. Open the Organize menu.
3. Select Remove Unwanted Index Tag.
4. Highlight the index tag you plan to remove, INTEREST, and then press ⏎Enter.

Objective 6: To Edit a Database with an Index in Control

Browsing through a database and editing records can be difficult when those records are not in any meaningful sequence. Remember that records in a database are on disk in the order in which the records were entered. The last name Mitchell might appear after the last name Simpson. If you edit with an index in control, such as a last name index, you can find records as easily as looking up a name or business in the phone book. All indexes update without any action on your part. If you change one of the record keys when your database is under the control of an index, however, you must indicate which record is now current.

To edit your database with an index in control, activate the index you want (or create an index if one does not exist). Then access Browse mode. The only difference between editing a field under the control of an index and editing any other field involves the cursor location after the edit.

101

Editing a Non-Controlling Field in an Indexed Record

Suppose that you have a membership database under the control of an index on the last name and you need to change only the first name information for several members. Scroll through the alphabetical listing of names to find the first record that needs editing.

To edit a record by changing any field except the controlling field, simply navigate in Browse mode to the record needing change, and then enter the change. When you change the entry for a non-controlling field, the order of the records does not change.

The record you have just changed—the one on which the cursor is resting—is the current record. If you move the cursor from the current record by pressing ⬇, the next record becomes the current record, and you continue to browse your way through the alphabetical listing. The field being changed is not controlled by the active index, and *you* control cursor movement.

Editing a Controlling Field in an Indexed Record

Suppose instead that you need to edit the LAST_NAME field for several members after a rash of June weddings—changing Bell to Pell and Love to Swenson. Scroll through the records organized alphabetically on last name and change the Bell record. As soon as you move the cursor off the record just changed, all indexes are updated, and the changed record appears in its new location in the file—in this case, in the P's (for Pell). The cursor follows the revised record to its new location and advances to the next record, Reed in this example. It's a long way back to the letter *L* for the next change, Love.

The Record menu on the Browse or Edit screen enables you to make changes to your records. One of the change options is Follow Record to New Position. When the option is set to Yes, a changed record appears in its new indexed position. If the option is set to No, the records that previously surrounded the changed record continue to display.

Exercise 6.1: Changing the Follow Record to New Position Option

To change the Follow Record to New Position option and edit a field under control of an index, follow these steps:

1. Open a database, MEMBERS, under the control of an index on the field you want to change, and then access the Browse work surface.

2. Press (Alt) + (R) to select the Record option from the Menu bar.

3. Select Follow Record to New Position from the Record menu if the current setting is not the setting you want (otherwise, press (Esc)).

   If the Follow Record to New Position option had been set to Yes, it is set to No after you choose the option. If the option had been set to No, it is set to Yes after you choose the option.

4. After the menu disappears, position the cursor, and edit the field under the control of an index, changing *Bell* to *Pell*.

Figure 4.18 shows the BILL_LNAME field changed from Bell to Pell when the Follow record to new position option is set to No. Notice that the cursor remains where the Bell record was originally located. The cursor does not follow the changed record to its new location.

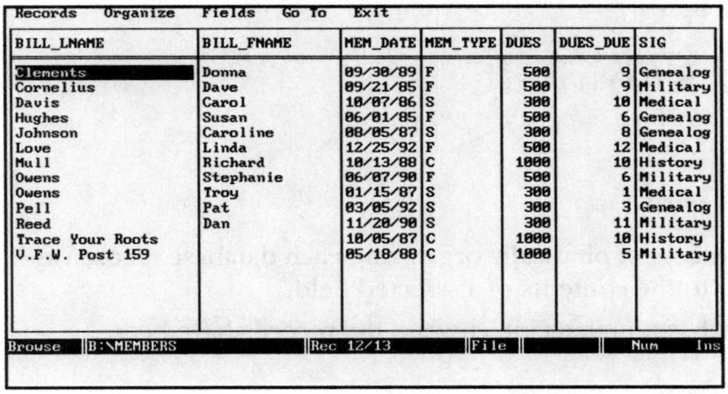

```
Records    Organize    Fields    Go To    Exit

BILL_LNAME          BILL_FNAME     MEM_DATE MEM_TYPE DUES  DUES_DUE SIG

Clements            Donna          09/30/89 F         500         9 Genealog
Cornelius           Dave           09/21/85 F         500         9 Military
Davis               Carol          10/07/86 S         300        10 Medical
Hughes              Susan          06/01/85 F         500         6 Genealog
Johnson             Caroline       08/05/87 S         300         8 Genealog
Love                Linda          12/25/92 F         500        12 Medical
Mull                Richard        10/13/88 C        1000        10 History
Owens               Stephanie      06/07/90 F         500         6 Military
Owens               Troy           01/15/87 S         300         1 Medical
Pell                Pat            03/05/92 S         300         3 Genealog
Reed                Dan            11/20/90 S         300        11 Military
Trace Your Roots                   10/05/87 C        1000        10 History
V.F.W. Post 159                    05/18/88 C        1000         5 Military



Browse    B:\MEMBERS           Rec 12/13      File              Num   Ins
```

Fig. 4.18
Setting the Follow Record to New Position option to No.

Figure 4.19 shows the same database with the same change but with the Follow Record to New Position option set to Yes.

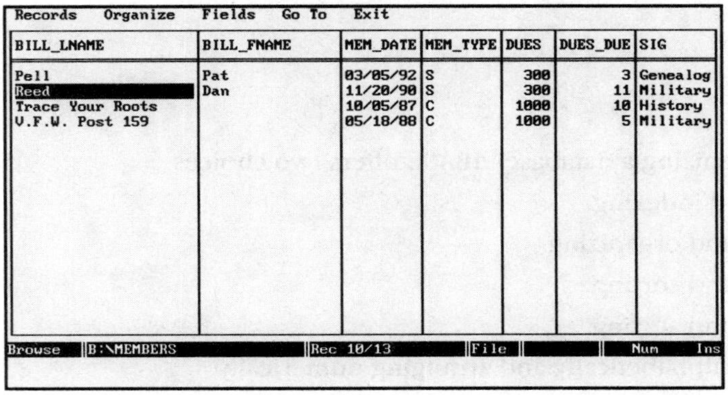

```
Records    Organize    Fields    Go To    Exit

BILL_LNAME          BILL_FNAME     MEM_DATE MEM_TYPE DUES  DUES_DUE SIG

Pell                Pat            03/05/92 S         300         3 Genealog
Reed                Dan            11/20/90 S         300        11 Military
Trace Your Roots                   10/05/87 C        1000        10 History
V.F.W. Post 159                    05/18/88 C        1000         5 Military



Browse    B:\MEMBERS           Rec 10/13      File              Num   Ins
```

Fig. 4.19
Setting the Follow Record to New Position option to Yes.

103

Chapter Summary

In this chapter you explored dBASE IV's options for arranging records in a meaningful sequence.

You are learning a great deal about dBASE IV as a database management system (DBMS). The three basic elements to managing any database are creating, maintaining, and using it. At this point, you should feel comfortable about the first two elements because you have created databases and indexes and have modified (or deleted) data, indexes, and database structures. The fun part is using the database—either to output your records in a meaningful sequence or to retrieve information selectively. You explored rearranging your records with indexes in this chapter; you start searching for selected data in Chapter 5.

Testing Your Knowledge

True/False Questions

1. Sorting is the process of physically organizing each database record on a disk according to the contents of a selected field.
2. The original database remains intact when the records have been sorted.
3. You can create indexes when you create or modify the database structure.
4. Indexes are stored in DBF files, and databases are stored in MDX files.
5. Using a multiple-index key, you can reorder records on more than one field.

Multiple Choice Questions

1. In terms of organizing a database, dBASE offers two choices:
    A. sorting and indexing.
    B. indexing and organizing.
    C. selecting and sorting.
    D. querying and sorting.
    E. arranging alphabetically and arranging numerically.

2. One advantage to a sort is that
    A. sorting the file requires more time than indexing.
    B. the results of a sort are placed in another file.
    C. it requires more disk space.
    D. you can have several keys, mixing data types.
    E. the sorted file requires a different name.

3. The item on the Create New Index Menu that requires completion is
    A. Order of Index.
    B. Name of Index.
    C. Index Expression.
    D. Display First Duplicate Key Only.
    E. both B and C.

4. If four records contain Apple, Apple, Orange, Orange, in the field named Fruit and this field is indexed using the display duplicate field key, only the following displays:
    A. Apple, Apple, Orange, Orange.
    B. Apple, Orange, Orange, Apple.
    C. Apple, Orange, Apple, Orange.
    D. Apple, Orange.
    E. Apple, Apple, Apple, Apple, Orange, Orange, Orange, Orange.

5. Using the UPPER( ) function with Happy, happy, HAPPY as data produces
    A. happy, Happy, HAPPY.
    B. happy, HAPPY, Happy.
    C. HAPPY, Happy, happy.
    D. HAPPY, happy, Happy.
    E. HAPPY.

Fill-in-the-Blank Questions

1. A(n) _____ key is a field on which to organize records.
2. Database records organized with a(n) _____ are not physically stored.
3. A(n) _____ on the Organize screen is a list of fields in the database.

4. The index _____ describes how dBASE makes the new index.

5. Indexes are stored in a(n) _____ file with the same name as the _____ file.

Review: Short Projects

1. Sorting a File

   Select the Inventory catalog and the Products database. Sort the file on the product code field, save the sorted file as Code, and print the sorted file.

2. Creating an Index

   Select the Equipment database located in the Inventory catalog, and print a quick report of the database. Set indexes on the fields, type of equipment, and date of purchase. Print a quick report of the indexed file.

3. Removing an Index

   Select the Equipment database, remove each index, and sort the file by using type of equipment and date of purchase.

Review: Long Projects

1. Sorting a File and Creating an Index

   Select the Lessons catalog and the database Cars. Sort the database on last name and first name, and save the sorted file as Lname. Display the structure of the database, and index the last name and first name fields. Print the indexed database.

2. Creating Multiple Indexes

   Select the Class catalog, and retrieve the Student database. Create multiple indexes, using social security, name, and instructor fields. Print the indexed database. Remove the social security index. Print the indexed database.

Conducting Simple Searches from the Data Panel

Y ou can use a great deal of time setting up and maintaining a database—time spent determining the file structure and entering or editing the contents of the records. Your efforts are rewarded, however, when you can quickly rearrange your records into a meaningful sequence or successfully search your database. This chapter discusses simple searches—those searches you complete by using only the Data panel in the dBASE IV Control Center.

Imagine that you work for a wholesale mail-order firm that maintains an inventory database including data fields for catalog number, type, model, unit of measure, retail price, quantity on hand, and manufacturer. You already know that you can index database contents, but think about why you might want to search through these records. Perhaps you need to update the retail price of one item, reduce the quantity on hand of another item, or find all items made by a particular manufacturer. Most database searches begin when you decide to edit records or find all records that meet specific criteria.

If you use options from the Data panel in the Control Center, you can go to specific records based on record location or field contents. You can go to record number 500, skip to every 10th record, search forward in the database for any record in which the manufacturer is General Supply, or search backward for the record containing the catalog number AC415, for example.

Think of a search limited to the Data panel as a maintenance search. You want to look at the data in general or make changes to selected records without printing custom reports or labels. After you learn the basic search procedures possible from the Data panel of the Control Center, you can try the expanded capabilities set up through the Query panel (see Chapter 6).

5

Objectives

1. To Position the Record Pointer
2. To Search Non-Indexed Fields
3. To Use Alternatives to Exact-Match Searches
4. To Search on an Indexed Field

Key Terms Used in This Chapter	
Match capitalization	The requirement that both upper- and lowercase letters must match in both field content and the search criterion.
Record number	A unique number assigned by dBASE IV to a record as it is added to the database.
Record pointer	An internal dBASE IV index file, separate from the database, that stores the sequence of numbers pointing to where the records are stored in the database.
Search string	A user-specified search condition for accessing selected records in a database.
Wild card	One of two symbols used to represent a variety of characters. The asterisk (*) wild card stands for one or more characters; the question mark (?) wild card stands for any single character.

Objective 1: To Position the Record Pointer

A record number in a database uniquely identifies each record, much as a Social Security number identifies an individual. dBASE IV internally keeps track of each new record by assigning it the next sequential number in ascending order. The number serves as a pointer to the record. The most simple database search you can make involves finding a record according to its record number.

As you look at your database in Browse or Edit mode, you can access records by using the cursor-control keys and the Go To menu options to scroll through the database—moving quickly to the first or last record, going directly to a particular record number, or skipping over a specified number of records.

5

Understanding the Current Record Pointer

When you look at records in Browse mode, the highlight bar rests on one field in the current record. If you switch to Edit mode, you see only the current record on-screen. dBASE IV points to the current record by its record number and displays that number in the status bar. The status bar in figure 5.1, for example, indicates that the current record is record 7. In addition to the record number, the status bar shows the total number of records in the database (13 in fig. 5.1).

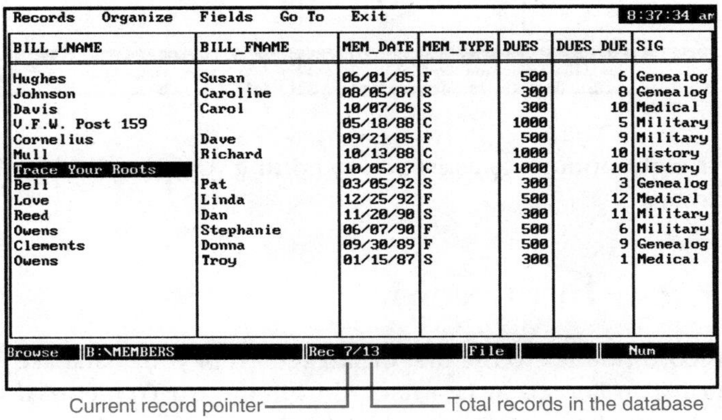

Records	Organize	Fields	Go To	Exit			8:37:34 am
BILL_LNAME		BILL_FNAME	MEM_DATE	MEM_TYPE	DUES	DUES_DUE	SIG
Hughes		Susan	06/01/85	F	500	6	Genealog
Johnson		Caroline	08/05/87	S	300	8	Genealog
Davis		Carol	10/07/86	S	300	10	Medical
V.F.W. Post 159			05/18/88	C	1000	5	Military
Cornelius		Dave	09/21/85	F	500	9	Military
Mull		Richard	10/13/88	C	1000	10	History
Trace Your Roots			10/05/87	C	1000	10	History
Bell		Pat	03/05/92	S	300	3	Genealog
Love		Linda	12/25/92	F	500	12	Medical
Reed		Dan	11/20/90	S	300	11	Military
Owens		Stephanie	06/07/90	F	500	6	Military
Clements		Donna	09/30/89	F	500	9	Genealog
Owens		Troy	01/15/87	S	300	1	Medical

| Browse | B:\MEMBERS | | Rec 7/13 | | File | | Num |

Current record pointer———————— Total records in the database

Fig. 5.1

The status bar displays the current record's number and the total number of records.

Using the Go To Menu To Position the Record Pointer

The Go To menu is your window to a variety of techniques for positioning the current record pointer and locating groups of related records.

Exercise 1.1: Accessing the Go To Menu

To access the Go To menu, follow these steps:

1. Access the Browse mode or Edit mode for the file you intend to search. The current database should be MEMBERS.

2. Press [Alt]+[G] to position the cursor on the Go To option in the menu bar at the top of the screen. The Go To menu appears, as shown in figure 5.2.

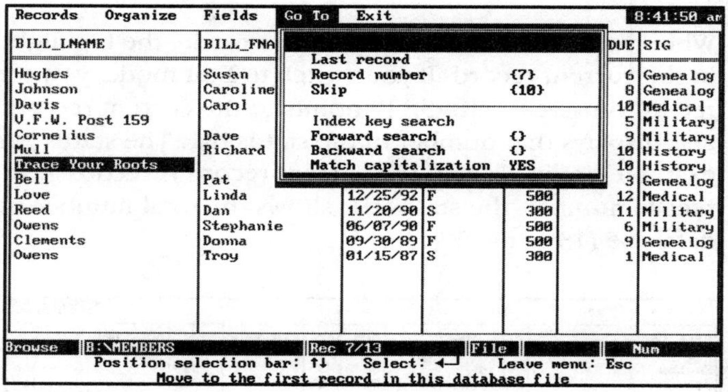

Fig. 5.2
The Go To menu.

The Go To menu offers eight options to assist you in editing your data and conducting simple searches.

Moving to the First or Last Record

To move the current record pointer to the first or last record of your database quickly, select the option Top Record or Last Record from the Go To menu. If no index is active, you see the first or last record in the database according to the record numbers. If an index is in control, you see the first or last record according to the way the records are reordered.

110

Exercise 1.2: Finding the First or Last Record

To position the record pointer on the first record in the database, follow these steps:

1. Access the Go To pull-down menu.

2. Press ⟨T⟩ to go to the top record of the database. After the record pointer is repositioned, the Go To pull-down menu disappears (see fig. 5.3).

```
Records   Organize   Fields   Go To   Exit                8:44:35 am

BILL_LNAME          BILL_FNAME     MEM_DATE MEM_TYPE DUES  DUES_DUE SIG

Hughes              Susan          06/01/85 F         500        6 Genealog
Johnson             Caroline       08/05/87 S         300        8 Genealog
Davis               Carol          10/07/86 S         300       10 Medical
V.F.W. Post 159                    05/18/88 C        1000        5 Military
Cornelius           Dave           09/21/85 F         500        9 Military
Mull                Richard        10/13/88 C        1000       10 History
Trace Your Roots                   10/05/87 C        1000       10 History
Bell                Pat            03/05/92 S         300        3 Genealog
Love                Linda          12/25/92 F         500       12 Medical
Reed                Dan            11/20/90 S         300       11 Military
Owens               Stephanie      06/07/90 F         500        6 Military
Clements            Donna          09/30/89 F         500        9 Genealog
Owens               Troy           01/15/87 S         300        1 Medical

Browse   B:\MEMBERS           Rec 1/13         File          Num
```

Fig. 5.3
The record pointer in the status bar indicates that record 1 is the current record.

To position the record pointer on the last record in the database, complete a process similar to that for finding the first record in the database: access the Go To pull-down menu, and press **L** to select Last record.

Using the Record Number To Find a Record

If you know the number of the record you want to make the current record, you can use the Record Number option on the Go To menu to move to that record. You also can use this option to look around your database. To look through records, for example, you can indicate a record number such as 300 and use the cursor-control keys to view surrounding records.

Exercise 1.3: Finding a Record by Its Number

To position the record pointer on a specific record number, access the Browse or Edit screen and then follow these steps:

1. Access the Go To pull-down menu.
2. Select Record Number. When prompted to enter the record number, type the record number of your choice, *3* for this exercise, and press ⏎Enter.

If you typed *3* as the requested record number, the record pointer in the status bar indicates that record 3 is the current record. It appears as the first record at the top of the screen.

Skipping Records

You can move forward or backward, skipping a specific number of records. Just use the Skip option on the Go To menu to move the pointer at set intervals.

Exercise 1.4: Skipping a Specified Number of Records

To shift the record pointer to positions at set intervals, access the Browse or Edit screen, and then follow these steps:

1. Access the Go To pull-down menu.
2. Press S to select Skip (see fig. 5.4).

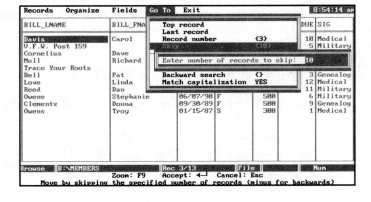

Fig. 5.4
The Skip option.

3. Type the skip interval of your choice, and then press ⏎Enter. Entering a positive number moves the record pointer forward in records; entering a negative number moves the record pointer backward in records.

112

Objective 2: To Search Non-Indexed Fields

Two problems can occur if you try to search for records in a large database by using only the Record Number and Skip options from the Go To menu to position the record pointer. First, you are unlikely to memorize which record number is associated with each record's content. In addition, you may find that using only cursor-control keys is a time-consuming way to move about when looking for a specific record.

If you know some information about the records you want to search for, such as a name or Social Security number, however, use the Forward Search and Backward Search options on the Go To menu. Both forward and backward searches work the same. The only difference is the direction of the search and the order in which records are found.

You must furnish a search condition, such as a Social Security number. If your search condition is specific enough, you can find the record on the first try. If the search condition is more general, however, such as the last name *Smith*, you may find the first of several records. After you find the first record meeting the search condition, keep pressing ⬆Shift+F3 (Previous) or ⬆Shift+F4 (Next) to find the remaining occurrences.

Searching Forward

The forward search begins to check records as soon as you select the Forward Search option and continues to search each record until finding one that matches the search string.

When you invoke the Forward Search command more than once, dBASE IV leaves the most recent search criterion on-screen and duplicates it in the Backward Search option. You can type a new search condition or edit the old search string.

Exercise 2.1: Executing a Forward Search

To execute a forward search, follow these steps:

1. Access the Browse mode or Edit mode of the MEMBERS database.
2. Position the cursor in the field SIG.
3. Press Alt+ G to open the Go To pull-down menu.

113

4. Press F to select Forward Search.

   A pop-up box appears, prompting you to enter the search string.

5. Type the search string **Genealogy**, as shown in figure 5.5. You must type the search criterion exactly as the data appears in the database, including capitalization.

5

Fig. 5.5
Enter the search
criterion.

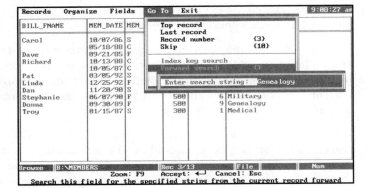

6. Press ↵Enter.

   The forward search stops on the first record that meets the search criterion you entered.

7. Press ⇧Shift + F4 to search for the next record that meets the search criterion.

Continue to press ⇧Shift + F4 to find the next record (or press ⇧Shift + F3 to find the previous record) that meets the search criterion.

Forward searching wraps around past the last database record, back to the first record, and continues in an infinite loop as long as you press the search key combination ⇧Shift + F4. If the search finds no records, you hear a beep and see the message Not Found. The error message box indicates that no records in the database meet the search criterion.

Searching Backward

The Backward Search option performs much like Forward search. The difference involves the direction of the search. The search moves backward to the top of the database, wraps around to the end of the database, and then continues in an infinite loop if two or more records are found. After you find the first of the records meeting the search condition, keep pressing ⇧Shift + F3 (Previous) to find the remaining occurrences.

Exercise 2.2: Executing a Backward Search

To execute a backward search, follow these steps:

1. Access the Browse mode or Edit mode of the MEMBERS database.
2. Position the cursor in the SIG field.
3. Open the Go To pull-down menu.
4. Press B to select Backward Search. A pop-up box appears.
5. In the pop-up box, type the search string Medical and then press
   ↵Enter.

The backward search stops on the first record that meets the search criterion you entered—before the point in the database where the search began. Continue to press ⇧Shift+F3 to search for the previous record that meets the search criterion (or press ⇧Shift+F4 to search for the next record that meets the search criterion). If the search finds no records, you hear a beep and see the message Not Found.

5

Objective 3: To Use Alternatives to Exact-Match Searches

You can see that Forward Search and Backward Search are more precise tools for finding data than the cursor-control keys and menu options that simply position the current record pointer. Having to enter the exact search string is limiting, however. If you use two dBASE IV features, wild cards and the Match capitalization option set to NO, you can avoid having to ensure that the search condition and the field contents match exactly.

Using Wild Cards

dBASE IV permits you to use two wild cards—symbols that tell dBASE IV to accept a variety of characters—when specifying a search string. The asterisk (*) wild card represents one or more characters; the question mark (?) wild card represents any single character. You can use wild cards to make search criteria more flexible.

You can use the wild card at the front of a search string as well as in the middle or at the end. Suppose that you recall only the name of a street address (for example, Cape), but not the house number. You can conduct a

search of address fields based on the search string *Cape* and find all records
in which the street address is on Cape Drive. You also find other addresses
such as any house number on Caper Lane or Capella Avenue.

Exercise 3.1: Using the * Wild Card

To search a database on the partial contents of a field, access the Browse
mode or Edit mode of the CARS database and follow these steps:

1. Position the cursor in the field to be searched, STREET, access the Go
   To pull-down menu, and press F to select Forward Search.
2. When prompted, type the search string *Cape* (see fig. 5.6).

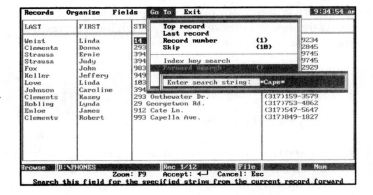

Fig. 5.6

A search for street
addresses contain-
ing the characters
Cape.

3. Press ↵Enter.

   The first record found by the search string *Cape* includes an address
   on Cape Dr.
4. Press ⇧Shift + F4.

The search string *Cape* next finds an address on Capella Ave. because the
address contains the characters *Cape*.

If you find more records than you want, try to restrict the scope of the wild
card by specifying additional letters. If you know the address you seek includes the word *Drive*, for example, type the search string *Cape Dr*. By
including *Dr* in the search string, you eliminate lanes, circles, roads, and so
on. As an alternative, type the search string *Cape *. Adding the space at the
end of *Cape* restricts the search to the whole word *Cape*.

Use the ? wild card to replace single characters in search strings. If you are not sure whether the phone number field in the record you seek is (317)123-4567 or (317)133-4567, for example, specify a search criterion of **(317)1?3-4567**. You can mix both wild cards to make the most flexible search criteria.

Exercise 3.2: Using Combination Wild Cards

To search a database by using a combination of wild cards in a search condition, follow these steps:

1. Position the cursor in the STREET field, access the Go To pull-down menu, and then press ⎡F⎤ to select Forward Search.

2. At the prompt, type the search string *Ca?e * (see fig. 5.7).

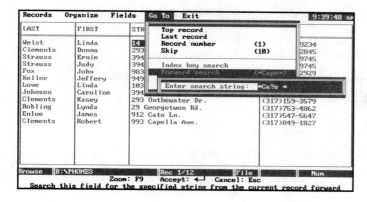

Fig. 5.7
A combination of wild cards used in the search string.

3. Press ⎡↵Enter⎤.

   The search string *Ca?e * causes dBASE IV to search for street addresses containing four-character combinations, such as *Cape*, *Cane*, or *Cate*. The first record found is record 4 with the street address Cave.

4. Press ⎡⇧Shift⎤+ ⎡F4⎤.

The search next finds a record with the street address Cape.

You may on occasion locate more records than you want to see. With a little practice in creating search strings, however, you can limit unwanted records retrieved by forward and backward searches.

In a forward or backward search, dBASE IV treats capital letters and lowercase letters differently. The letters *A* and *a* are two different letters to the computer. For purposes of your search, however, they are the same.

117

Using the Match Capitalization Option

The last option on the Go To menu is Match Capitalization. The options are YES and NO. The default setting is YES. When capitalization is set to YES, the characters in the search string must match the contents of the record, including capitalization. You may not find all addresses on Cape Drive if you do not capitalize the street name when it is added to the database (that is, if you type *cape*, not *Cape*).

If you select Match Capitalization on the Go To menu and set the option to NO, subsequent searches treat upper- and lowercase characters the same. A dBASE IV search operation then treats *123 Cape Dr* like *123 cape dr*. When you want to use the Match Capitalization option, set it prior to each search.

Exercise 3.3: Using Match Capitalization

To use the Match Capitalization option, access the CARS database, choose the Browse mode or Edit mode, and then follow these steps:

1. Position the cursor in the STREET field, and open the Go To menu.
2. If Match Capitalization displays YES, press M to switch the setting to NO.
3. Press F to select Forward Search.
4. Type the search string CAPE and then press ↵Enter.

Because the search is no longer case-sensitive, the first record found contains the address 3940 cave Cir., as shown in figure 5.8.

Fig. 5.8
The search is
no longer
case-sensitive.

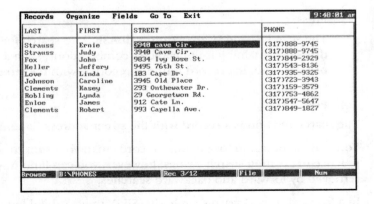

Continue to browse through the database by using the ⟨⇧Shift⟩+⟨F4⟩ (Next) and ⟨⇧Shift⟩+⟨F3⟩ (Previous) keys. Notice that capitalization is no longer a factor in finding records. This feature is particularly useful if data has been entered with case errors.

Remember that Forward Search and Backward Search are improvements over simply positioning the current record pointer in order to find a specific record. Include wild cards in search criteria and set Match Capitalization to NO to create even more powerful searches.

Objective 4: To Search on an Indexed Field

If you plan to search a field frequently (such as a last name field), you may want to create an index on that field and activate the index before you use the Go To menu. If you do, the option Index Key Search is available. First, you see the index expression used to create the index. Then you are asked to enter the data for which you want the index searched.

The search is rapid, and you see each record whose index key matches the search condition you entered. As your database gets larger, the speed of Index Key Search is impressively faster than Forward Search or Backward Search because related sets of records are grouped.

You should not use the ⟨⇧Shift⟩+⟨F3⟩ (Previous) and ⟨⇧Shift⟩+⟨F4⟩ (Next) keys when you use Index Key Search because the cursor may jump three or four records. Because the related records are grouped, however, you can use the ⟨↑⟩ and ⟨↓⟩ keys to access each of the records found.

Activating an Index before a Search

Before using the Index Key Search option, activate the appropriate index. (If the index does not exist, create it. You create an index by using Create New Index on the Organize menu of the Database Design or Browse or Edit work surface.)

Exercise 4.1: Activating an Existing Index

To activate an existing index, access the MEMBERS database, enter the Browse mode or Edit mode, and follow these steps:

119

1. Press ⌐Alt⌐+ ⌐O⌐ to access the Organize pull-down menu.
2. Press ⌐O⌐ to select Order Records by Index (see fig. 5.9).

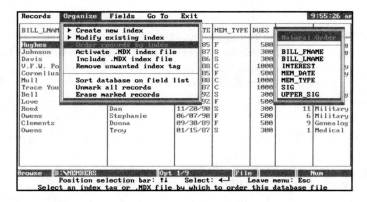

Fig. 5.9
A list of all indexes
in the master
index file (MDX)
appears.

3. Press ⌐↑⌐ and ⌐↓⌐ to highlight the appropriate index in the list that
   appears, and then press ⌐┘Enter⌐ to put that index in control of the
   database.

   With BILL_LNAME selected as the controlling index, the database
   automatically reappears in alphabetical order by last name, as shown
   in figure 5.10.

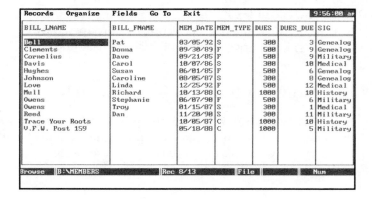

Fig. 5.10
The BILL_LNAME
index is in control
of the database.

Writing Search Criteria

When you choose the Index Key Search option on the Go To menu, a window
opens on-screen, and a flashing cursor in the highlighted area prompts you to

enter the search string. Keep the following items in mind as you write the search criterion:

- If the index expression was created with the UPPER( ) function, the string you search for must be uppercase. The expression UPPER(NAME) requires that you search for MARIANNE, for example, not Marianne.

- You can enter a partial search string representing the first characters in the index. For the expression UPPER(FIRSTNAME), you can search for MAR rather than MARIANNE. Do not be too brief. MAR also can find names like MARK, MARCELLA, and MARCUS.

- The Match Capitalization option is not effective in index-key searches. Your index should use the UPPER( ) function, and your search string should be all capital letters.

- Wild-card characters are not available in index-key searches.

- An index that combines two fields, such as UPPER(STATE+CITY), does not permit you to find all the cities named PORTLAND because you can enter only a partial search string representing the first characters in the city name. You have to create an index for just the city field in order to search for the city PORTLAND.

Exercise 4.2: Writing an Index-Key Search String

To write an index-key search string, open the MEMBERS database, access the Browse mode or Edit mode, and then follow these steps:

1. Position the cursor in the BILL_LNAME field and then press Alt + G to access the Go To menu.

2. Press I to select the Index Key Search option. A prompt appears, asking you to enter a search condition applicable to the current controlling index.

3. Type the search string Owens to locate all records whose BILL_LNAME field contains the last name Owens.

4. Press ↵Enter to return to the Browse mode or Edit mode. The cursor automatically positions itself on the first record that meets the search condition.

5. Use ↓ and ↑ to scroll to other records meeting the search condition.

Records that meet the index-key search condition are found quickly because they already are grouped according to the index controlling the database.

Chapter Summary

In this chapter you explored dBASE IV's options to conduct simple searches from the Data panel. All searches for database contents were initiated by using eight Go To menu options accessed from the Browse or Edit work surface.

You can perform most simple searches through the Data panel of the dBASE IV Control Center, as discussed in this chapter. You may need to create search criteria, however, that will be used by other Control Center panels, such as the Report or Labels panel. dBASE IV provides extensive search capabilities in the Query panel options presented in the next chapter.

5

Testing Your Knowledge

True/False Questions

1. A record number in a database uniquely identifies each record.
2. The record pointer in the status bar indicates the field number of the record.
3. The only difference between the forward and backward searches is the direction of the search and the order in which records are found.
4. The asterisk (*) wild card represents any single character.
5. You can enter a partial search string representing a certain number of characters in the index.

Multiple Choice Questions

1. The most simple search you can make of your database involves
   A. first sorting the database.
   B. finding a record according to its record number.
   C. finding a record according to the major index.
   D. first sorting the database and then selecting a record.
   E. typing the exact match needed.

2. Accessing the Go To pull-down menu and pressing ⊤
    A. takes you to the last record in the database.
    B. takes you to the records that begin with a *T*.
    C. takes you to the top record of the database.
    D. takes you to the middle record of the database.
    E. requests the record number needed.

3. The forward search begins to check records as soon as you select the
    A. Backward Search option.
    B. Top Record option.
    C. Last Record option.
    D. Forward Search option.
    E. Skip option.

4. The symbols that indicate a variety of characters in specifying a search string are
    A. / and @
    B. * and ?
    C. \ and /
    D. ~ and *
    E. * and .

5. If the index expression was created with the UPPER( ) function, the string you search for must be
    A. both upper- and lowercase.
    B. lowercase.
    C. started with an uppercase character.
    D. started with a lowercase character.
    E. uppercase.

Fill-in-the-Blank Questions

1. When you look at records in _____ mode, the highlighted bar rests on one field in the _____ record.

2. Entering a positive number moves the record pointer _____ in records; entering a negative number moves the record pointer _____ in records.

5

3. If no records are found in the search, you hear a _____ and see the message _____.

4. You can use the _____ card at the front of a search string as well as in the _____ or at the end.

5. In a forward or backward search, dBASE IV treats _____ letters and _____ letters differently.

Review: Short Projects

1. Positioning the Record Cursor

   Access the Cars database from the Lesson catalog. Open the Go To menu, find the first and last records, and then use the Skip selection.

2. Searching a Database

   Access the Student database from the Class catalog. Use the forward search to find a record. Use the backward search to find the same record. Practice typing the correct string and then an invalid string.

3. Using Wild-Card Searches

   Use wild cards to search the Product database in the Inventory catalog. Use the Quick Report to print the database, and then use a wild-card search. Print the screen of the selected records.

Review: Long Projects

1. Positioning the Record Cursor and Sorting a Database

   Access the Inventory catalog and Equipment database, find every third record, and print the screen displaying each record. Add five additional records. Then sort the database, and name the sorted file **Sorteq**. Find every third record, and print the screen displaying each record.

2. Positioning the Record Cursor and Searching Indexed and Non-indexed Fields

   Access the Student database from the Class catalog. Add five additional records. Perform a forward search, using wild cards to find selected courses. Perform searches on an indexed and a non-indexed field. Print the database. Find every fourth record. Print the first record found, using Print Screen.

Creating Simple Queries

If your database is small and your information needs are simple, searching records from the Data panel's Browse or Edit screen (as described in the preceding chapter) may be adequate. If your database is larger, however, you may find setting up a query from the Queries panel on the Control Center more efficient. A query acts as a filter by limiting the display of records and fields.

As databases increase in size—in the number of fields (data items) and number of records—search criteria can become complex, extending search time dramatically. In a medical center's database of several thousand patients, for example, each record may contain more than 150 fields (name fields, complete address fields, physical description fields, prior medical history fields, and so on).

A query's search string can be quite complex, including calculations and multiple search conditions. Rather than merely seeking records by a single string (such as the name of the referring doctor), you might want to find the names and phone numbers of all patients who have the following characteristics: they are over 45 years old, have a family history of heart disease, and have not had an electrocardiogram within the last two years.

Setting up filtering conditions from the Control Center's Queries panel offers many advantages over simple searches from the Go To menu in Browse mode or Edit mode. If you establish a query, you can limit the Browse or Edit screen display to selected records (such as patients experiencing heart disease) and to specific fields within records (each patient's number, sex, age, and medication).

When you set up a query, you can rearrange the order of fields on the Browse or Edit screen and determine which fields and records are made available to Browse or Edit, Quick Report, Reports, and Labels operations. You can access data from more than one database or save a query to disk for later use.

Objectives

1. To Understand and Use a Query
2. To Work with a File Skeleton
3. To Work with a View Skeleton
4. To Make Simple Queries
5. To Save a Query

Key Terms Used in This Chapter	
File skeleton	The upper portion of the Query Design work surface in which the user must specify the field contents used to select records in a query operation.
Calculated fields	The left area in the middle portion of the Query Design work surface in which the user can define one or more fields that are not part of the database.
Condition box	The right area in the middle portion of the Query Design work surface in which the user can specify complex conditions involving several fields.
View skeleton	The lower portion of the Query Design work surface in which the user must specify the fields to display (on-screen or to the printer) from the records selected.
Filter	The Query process for hiding database records that do not match specified search criteria.
Operator	A symbol used in a query to select a record based on a variety of data matches or numeric conditions. An operator shows the relationship between data and search criteria.

Objective 1: To Understand and Use a Query

New users of dBASE IV might be intimidated by talk of filters, queries, file skeletons, and view skeletons. Rather than rely on narrative to introduce the topics, look at figures 6.1, 6.2, and 6.3, which transform an unfiltered view of a database into a view controlled by a query.

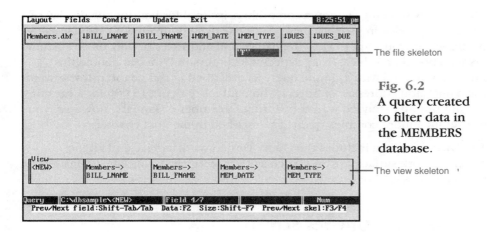

Fig. 6.1
All fields and all records in the MEMBERS database viewed in Browse mode.

Fig. 6.2
A query created to filter data in the MEMBERS database.

The file skeleton contains a search condition which limits records to those in which membership type is *F* (family).

The view skeleton limits display to four (of eight) fields; the fields are not in the order they appear in the database.

127

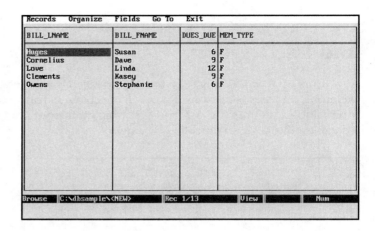

Fig. 6.3
MEMBERS
database in
Browse mode
under control of
a query: limited
fields and limited
records.

6

These figures depict the effect of a query on the Browse display; similar effects occur when a query is activated before running a custom report. The contents of the database have not changed. Only the view of database contents has been restricted. You can set up a variety of database filters through the Queries panel of the dBASE IV Control Center.

Using the Queries Screen

The Queries screen gives you a comprehensive tool for limiting the display of records and fields in your database. Suppose that you maintain a vehicle sales database and you want to view the names and addresses of only those customers who bought a vehicle from a specific salesperson. You can handle this information need with a simple query as described in this chapter. If you want the names and addresses of buyers who paid more than $15,000 for a car but did not buy an extended warranty during December or January, however, you can set up a more complex query, as described in the next chapter.

The Queries screen includes the Query Design work surface and all the common work-surface features, such as the menu bar, status bar, navigation line, and message line.

Accessing the Queries Screen

You can access the Queries screen from the Queries panel in the Control Center or from any other design work surface.

128

Exercise 1.1: Activating the Query Design Work Surface

To access a new Query Design work surface after specifying which database to open, follow these steps:

1. Access the dBASE IV Control Center.

2. Highlight the desired database name, MEMBERS, in the Data panel, press ⏎Enter, and select Use File.

3. Highlight Create in the Queries panel (see fig. 6.4).

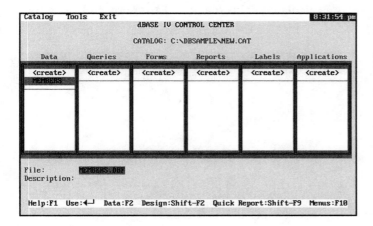

Fig. 6.4
The database MEMBERS appears above the horizontal line in the Data panel, indicating that the database is in use.

4. Press ⏎Enter. The Query Design work surface appears. The name of the associated database appears near the upper left corner (see fig. 6.5).

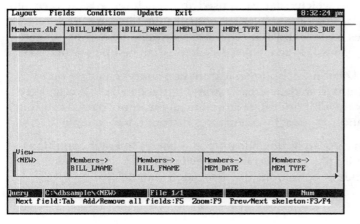

Name of the associated database

Fig. 6.5
The Query Design work surface.

Understanding the Query Design Work Surface

The Query Design work surface uses a query-by-example technique to help you find information in your databases. Indicating what information you want from your databases is like filling out a form. The Query Design work surface is that form, a graphic representation of your database.

The Query Design work surface is divided into three main sections. The upper portion of the work surface shows one or more file skeletons, and the lower portion of the screen displays the view skeleton. The middle section of the work surface may display a calculated fields (Calc'd Flds) box and a condition box (see fig. 6.6).

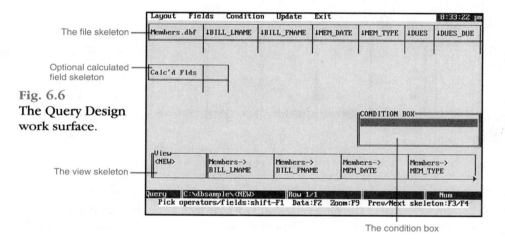

The file skeleton

Optional calculated field skeleton

Fig. 6.6
The Query Design work surface.

The view skeleton

The condition box

A file skeleton controls which database is used and which records are accessed in the database. The segment to the far left contains the file name. Field names follow the file names. Search and sort criteria are written in columns beneath the associated field names. Up to eight file skeletons can be open at one time.

A calculated fields skeleton (an optional feature in a query) enables you to create new information from data already stored in the database. A calculated field might multiply the unit price data stored in an inventory database by 0.05 to produce information about a 5 percent sales discount, for example.

You use a condition box (an optional feature in a query) to enter conditions that apply to the entire file. Use this box to specify complex conditions involving several fields or conditions not associated with fields.

A view skeleton controls which fields within records are used as output after database records are selected according to the search or sort conditions entered in the file skeletons. Each query has only one view skeleton.

Using the Queries Status Bar

The status bar at the bottom of the screen provides information about the Query Design work surface. Five segments appear across the status bar (see fig. 6.7).

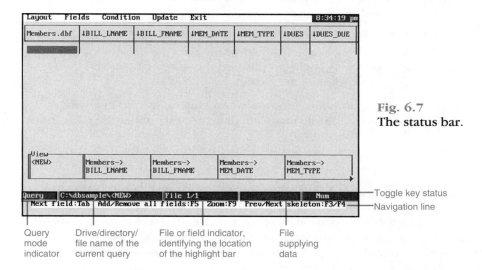

Fig. 6.7
The status bar.

6

Learning Keys To Use in Query Operations

Use the keys listed on the navigation line at the bottom of the screen to move around the Query Design work surface (refer to fig. 6.7). The navigation line is a dynamically changing help feature, and you must refer to it frequently because not all keys are active at the same time.

Press Tab↹ to move the highlight bar right one field within a skeleton (or press ⇧Shift + Tab↹ to move left one field).

Press F5 to move a field between skeletons. Press F9 to enlarge the view of the current highlighted field. Press F3 or F4 to move the highlight bar between skeletons.

Additional keys for moving around the work surface also are available:

*   Ctrl + PgUp moves quickly to the top of a file skeleton column.

*   Ctrl + PgDn moves quickly to the end of a file skeleton column.

*   Home and End move the highlight to the first or last field, respectively, in the current skeleton.

*   ← and → move the cursor left or right, respectively, within the highlight bar where specifications are typed.

*   ↑ and ↓ move the highlight bar up or down a line, respectively, in the field column.

*   F6 selects a field to be moved within the view skeleton.

*   F7 initiates moving a selected field within the view skeleton. (After pressing F7, press ← or → to position the selected field, and then press ↵Enter to complete the move.)

For additional instructions and prompts when moving around the work surface, watch the message line that sometimes appears under the navigation line.

Objective 2: To Work with a File Skeleton

A query requires at least one database to be active. In query jargon, the fields in the database you want to search form the file's *skeleton*. A *file skeleton* is just a listing across the top of the screen of all field names in the database. Up to eight file skeletons can be added to a single query; they also can be removed from a query.

Creating a File Skeleton

To set up one or more file skeletons on the Query Design work surface, highlight Create in the Queries panel before or after you open a database to use in the search. If you first open a database through the Data panel, the file skeleton appears automatically.

You also can create a query without first specifying a database. The sequence of steps is slightly different than if a database is in use, however.

Exercise 2.1: Working with the Query Design Work Surface

To select records with specific criteria, you need to create the criteria using the Query Design work surface. Follow these steps:

1. Access the dBASE IV Control Center (all file names in the Data panel should appear below the line, indicating that the files are closed).

2. Highlight Create on the Queries panel and press ⏎Enter. Because no database is in use, the Query Design work surface appears with the Layout pull-down menu selected automatically (see fig. 6.8).

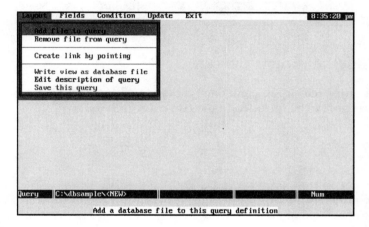

Fig. 6.8
The Query Design work surface.

3. Press ⏎Enter to select Add File to Query. A picklist window pops up in the upper right corner of your screen.

4. Highlight the name of the database to be used in the query file and then press ⏎Enter.

   The heading in the first column indicates the database name. The file skeleton arranges field names across the top portion of the Query Design work surface in the order the fields appear in the database (see fig. 6.9).

While a database is active, you can use the file skeleton area to restrict the records selected for output to screen or printer. If you want to find only those members who list genealogy as a special interest, for example, type **Genealogy** as the query specification in the column under the SIG heading. (Later sections provide an in-depth look at setting specifications.)

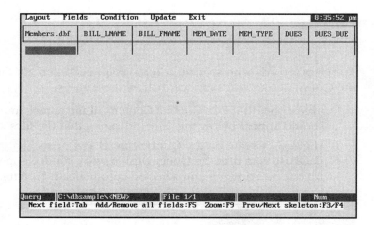

Fig. 6.9
The database
name and field
names in place.

Removing a File Skeleton

Remember that you can specify up to eight databases in the file skeleton, which controls the records to be included in the current search (query) operation.

Exercise 2.2: Removing a File Skeleton

To remove a file skeleton from the Query Design work surface, follow these steps:

1. Using the F3 (Prev) and F4 (Next), highlight the database name to be removed.
2. Press L to select the Layout menu. Highlight the Remove File from Query option (refer to fig. 6.8).
3. Press ↵Enter to remove the file skeleton.

If you remove the only file skeleton, you automatically see the Layout menu so that you can add a file to the work surface.

Objective 3: To Work with a View Skeleton

Remember that a file skeleton is just a listing across the upper portion of the screen of all field names in the database. For each query, dBASE IV also requires that you create a view skeleton—a list of fields across the lower portion of the screen, that determines the fields used in any query outputs to the screen or printer. Without a view skeleton, you cannot return to (or go to) one of the other work modes, such as Browse or Edit, Forms, Reports, or Labels.

To understand how to use a view skeleton, suppose that you are interested in viewing only the names and type of membership of members indicating a special interest in genealogy. You can limit the view skeleton to just the three fields BILL_LNAME, BILL_FNAME, and TYPE. Any output to the screen or printer is limited to only those records in which the special interest is genealogy (as specified in the file skeleton) and only those fields within each record that provide name and type of membership data (as specified in the view skeleton).

After you create a view skeleton, you can rearrange fields in the view and remove one or more fields from the view.

Creating a View Skeleton

You can create a view in one of two ways, both of which transfer field names from the file skeleton to the view skeleton. You can transfer all file skeleton field names to the view skeleton in one operation, or you can transfer field names one at a time.

Exercise 3.1: Transferring All Fields to the View Skeleton

To transfer all fields to the view skeleton, follow these steps:

1. Use `Tab⇥` or `⇧Shift`+`Tab⇥` to position the highlight on the MEMBERS database name.

    If you highlight a database name in the file skeleton, dBASE IV applies the next action to all fields in the associated skeleton.

2. Press `F5` (Fields) to create the view skeleton (see fig. 6.10).

To transfer a single field to the view skeleton, highlight the field name in the file skeleton and press `F5`. That key acts as a toggle switch for adding or removing all fields or a single field.

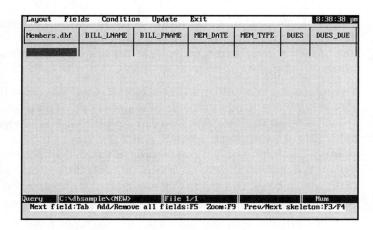

Fig. 6.10
dBASE copies all
field names from
the file skeleton
to the view
skeleton.

Removing Fields from the View Skeleton

dBASE IV makes removing a field name set up in the view skeleton easy.

Exercise 3.2: Removing a Field from the View Skeleton

To remove a field from the view skeleton, follow these steps:

1. Press F4 (Next) until the highlight is on the view skeleton at the bottom of the Query Design work surface. The highlight moves to the view skeleton and is positioned above the first field. If the highlight was positioned in the view skeleton previously, dBASE IV remembers the last field the highlight was on and automatically returns the highlight to that field.

2. Using Tab ⇆ or ⇧Shift + Tab ⇆, position the cursor on the MEM_DATE field, to be removed from the view (see fig. 6.11).

3. Press F5 to remove the field.

Generally, you do not include all fields in the view skeleton. The more fields in a database, the more likely you need only selected items for each separate query.

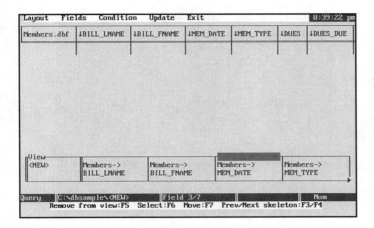

Fig. 6.11
The highlight is
positioned above
the MEM_DATE
field.

Moving Fields in a View Skeleton

If you add fields to the view skeleton one at a time, you can control the order of the fields. Frequently, however, you may need to rearrange the order of the fields already in the view skeleton.

Exercise 3.3: Moving Fields

After the fields are in the view, you can rearrange them easily by positioning the highlight in the view skeleton and following these steps:

1. Using `Tab↹` or `⇧Shift`+`Tab↹`, position the highlight on the field to be moved, MEM_TYPE.

2. Press `F6` to select the field to be moved. The field name is surrounded by a box (see fig. 6.12). To select two or more adjacent fields, use `Tab↹` and `⇧Shift`+`Tab↹` after pressing `F6`.

3. Press `↵Enter` to confirm the selection.

4. Press `F7` to choose the move operation.

5. Use `Tab↹` or `⇧Shift`+`Tab↹` to place the highlight bar where the selected field is to be moved.

6. Press `↵Enter` to complete the move (see fig. 6.13).

137

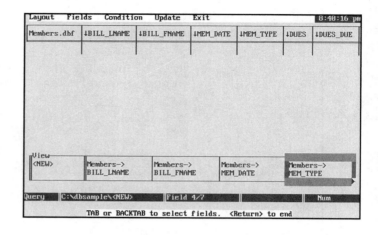

Fig. 6.12
The field to
be moved is
surrounded by
a box.

6

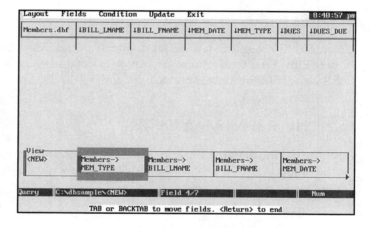

Fig. 6.13
The highlighted
field is positioned
at its new
location.

Now that you have learned to manage the file and view skeletons, the next
thing to do is specify the filter conditions that select the records you need
from the database.

Objective 4: To Make Simple Queries

Queries are filters that restrict what fields and records dBASE IV can access,
and they are used with other work surfaces, such as Data, Reports, and Labels.
Although you are searching the database for specific records, actually you are

setting a filter condition. That query or filter condition allows dBASE IV to access only those records that meet the criteria you specify. If you execute a custom report or edit records in the database, the screen appears as if the only records in the database were those that meet the search criteria. A query file, once activated, remains in control of the database until you close it, select another query at the Control panel, or exit dBASE IV.

The simplest query involves searching for records based on the content of a single field. After you create the appropriate file skeleton and view skeleton and enter the search criterion in the file skeleton, you can execute the query and store the specifications for the query on disk so that they can be used again.

Exercise 4.1: Making a Query

To begin any query, follow these steps:

1. Access the Control Center screen, select the database name, and then press ⏎Enter.
2. Highlight the Create option in the Queries panel and then press ⏎Enter.

You can search any type of data field, including a memo field, by specifying a search condition beneath the associated field name in the file skeleton (in the upper portion of the Query Design screen). Field types queried more often than others include character, numeric, logical, and date. Each data type has a few rules of its own for writing search criteria.

Locating Character Data

To perform a query on a character field, move the highlight bar (using Tab↹ or ⇧Shift + Tab↹) to the character field name in the Query Design work surface file skeleton. You then must type the search specification in quotation marks. *All character expressions must be enclosed in quotation marks*. To search a membership database for all records containing the last name Fox, for example, you would type "**Fox**" as the search condition. To produce a list of all cars sold to buyers in ZIP code 46321, you would enter "**46321**" under the ZIP code field in the file skeleton (that is, if the field was defined in the database structure as a character field).

Exercise 4.2: Finding Character Data

To create a query containing a character field filter and view the results in Browse mode, follow these steps:

1. Access the Query Design work surface for the database you want to search, CARS.

2. Transfer the desired field names to the view skeleton (see fig. 6.14).

3. Move the cursor to the appropriate field in the file skeleton, and type the character data you want to locate; in quotation marks: "Fox". Be sure to use correct capitalization.

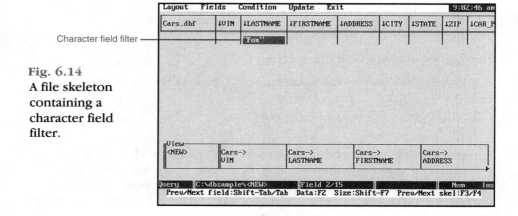

Character field filter ─

Fig. 6.14
A file skeleton containing a character field filter.

4. Press F2 (Data) to view the results in Browse mode (press F2 a second time, if necessary, to switch from Edit to Browse mode).

Be sure to double-check your criteria for spelling and capitalization.

The process for querying other data types is similar to that for querying character fields. Specifying criteria for each data type has a few idiosyncrasies, however.

Locating Numeric Data

Numeric criteria should be entered without quotation marks and using only numbers, one decimal point, and a minus sign (if necessary).

Exercise 4.3: Finding Numeric Data

To establish a query based on a numeric field and view the results in Browse mode, follow these steps:

1. Access the Query Design work surface for the database you want to search, CARS, and then transfer the desired field names to the view skeleton.

2. Move the cursor to the appropriate field in the file skeleton, and type the numeric data you want to locate: 12500 (see fig. 6.15). Do not use quotation marks.

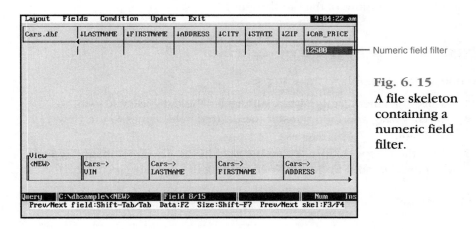

Numeric field filter

Fig. 6. 15
A file skeleton containing a numeric field filter.

3. Press F2 to see the results in Browse mode or Edit mode.

Remember that numeric fields contain only numbers, a decimal point, and a minus sign (if necessary). Do not use quotation marks, commas, or dollar signs. Following is a table showing valid numeric entries.

Valid	Invalid
100	$100
42563.27	42,567.00
–250	"–250"

Locating Logical Data

Logical fields can contain any of the following four entries to indicate a true condition:

.T.　.t.　.Y.　.y.

Logical fields can also contain any of the following four entries to indicate a false condition:

.F.　.f.　.N.　.n.

To query a logical field, you must enter one of the true or false indicators in the appropriate column of the file skeleton.

6

Exercise 4.4: Finding Logical Data

To find logical data, follow these steps:

1. Access the Query Design work surface for the database you want to search, CARS, and then transfer the desired field names to the view skeleton.
2. Move the cursor to the appropriate field in the file skeleton, and type the logical condition .N. for No, including the periods (see fig. 6.16).

Logical field filter —

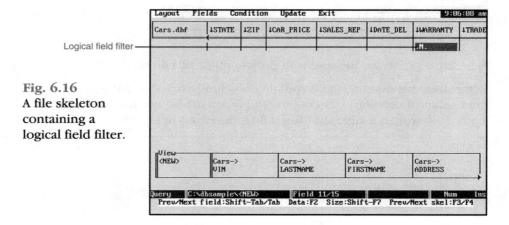

Fig. 6.16
A file skeleton containing a logical field filter.

3. Press F2 to see the results in the Browse mode or Edit mode.

Locating a Date

When entering a search criterion based on a date field, type the date in braces ({}) in the format mm/dd/yy. The braces indicate that a date is enclosed.

Exercise 4.5: Finding a Date

Follow these steps to search for a date specification:

1. Access the Query Design work surface for the database you want to search, CARS, and then transfer the desired field names to the view skeleton.

2. Move the cursor to the appropriate field in the file skeleton, and type the date you want to locate: {07/25/92} (see fig. 6.17).

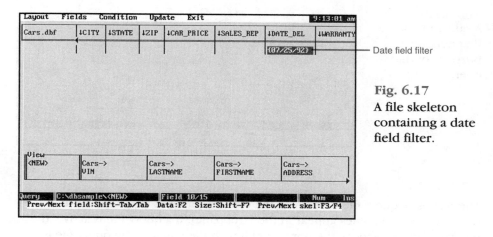

Date field filter

Fig. 6.17
A file skeleton containing a date field filter.

3. Press F2 to see the results in Browse mode or Edit mode.

Objective 5: To Save a Query

If you find that you execute a particular query on a regular basis, you can save the query specifications for recall at a later date. You provide a name containing up to eight characters; dBASE IV provides the QBE extension denoting a query file.

Exercise 5.1: Saving a Query

To save the query specifications set up in the file skeleton and view skeleton, follow these steps:

1. Press [Alt]+ [E] to access the Exit option on the Query Design menu bar.

2. Select Save Changes and Exit.

3. Type your choice of a name for the query file: ZIPCODE (see fig. 6.18).

6

Fig. 6.18
A query file name
that denotes the
purpose of the
query.

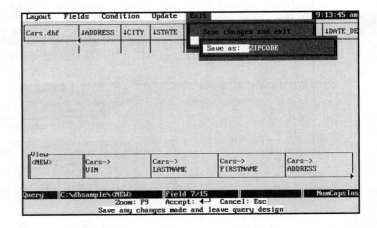

4. Press [↵Enter]

The names of query files appear in the Control panel in the same manner that database file names appear in the Data panel. If a query file is active, the file name appears above the horizontal line in the panel; if the query file is inactive, the file name appears below the horizontal line.

Chapter Summary

In this chapter, you learned about dBASE IV's Queries panel, through which you can facilitate searching a database by setting up a query. A query enables you to filter out unwanted records and to limit the number of fields displayed in the remain records.

The simple queries illustrated in this chapter are based on exact matches of character, numeric, logical, and date search conditions to data in the database. The next chapter illustrates more complex queries.

Testing Your Knowledge

True/False Questions

1. The Query Design work surface is divided into three main sections.
2. A file skeleton controls which fields are used and which records are accessed.
3. The Remove File from Query option removes the highlighted database from the current file skeleton.
4. Queries are filters that restrict which fields and records dBASE IV can access.
5. dBASE IV provides the extension QRY, denoting a query, to the file name selected.

Multiple Choice Questions

1. All the following are common work surface features on the Queries screen except the
   A. menu bar.
   B. status bar.
   C. navigation line.
   D. query design.
   E. message line.

2. To move the highlight bar one field right in the skeleton on the Query Design work surface, press
   A. ⇧Shift + Tab⇆.
   B. F4.
   C. Tab⇆.
   D. F9.
   E. F3.

145

3. In query jargon, the fields in the database that you want to search form the file's
   A. filter.
   B. query.
   C. template.
   D. record.
   E. skeleton.

4. Once you create a view skeleton, you can
   A. order fields on a descending key.
   B. rearrange fields in the view.
   C. remove one or more fields.
   D. copy records.
   E. both B and C.

5. To search a database for all records containing last name Jones, you would type what as the search condition?
   A. "Jones"
   B. "jones"
   C. Jones
   D. "JONES"
   E. JONES

Fill-in-the-Blank Questions

1. The Query Design _____ is a graphic representation of your database.

2. A _____ skeleton controls which database is used and which records are accessed in the database.

3. Queries are _____ that restrict what fields and _____ dBASE IV can access.

4. _____ criteria should be entered without quotation marks and use only numbers, one decimal point, and a minus sign if necessary.

5. When entering a search criteria based on a date field, type the _____ in _____ in the format _____.

Review: Short Projects

1. Creating a File Skeleton

   Create a file skeleton using the Inventory catalog to select your database files. Select Equipment and Product.

2. Using a View Skeleton

   Create a file and view skeleton for the Student database, and move selected fields.

3. Creating and Saving a Query

   Create and save a query using the Equipment database, and select records according to type of equipment.

Review: Long Projects

1. Creating Catalogs and Queries

   Create a catalog called BUSINESS. Create a database with the following fields and example data:

Code	Type	Artist Name	Title	Category	Price
B234	Tape	Pavarotti	Pavarotti in Concert	Opera	18.95
A123	CD	U-2	Rattle and Hum	Rock	27.95
A477	CD	DAS EFX	They Want EFX	Rap	21.95

   Add 10 records with common fields. Save the database as MUSIC.

   Create a second database, named CONTACTS, with the following fields:

LastName	City
FirstName	State
Title	ZIP
Company	Phone
Address1	Category
Address2	

147

The Category field should have the same contents as the Category field in the MUSIC database. Suppose that a company is interested in rock music. Create a query of all business contacts in which the Category field is equal to Rock. Save the query as ROCK. Print the screen of all contacts that meet this criteria.

2. Creating a Database and Saving a Query

Create a database of area restaurants. Be sure to have a field called CUISINE in the database. Save the database as RESTAURANT. Add 10 of your favorite restaurants. Create a query finding all the restaurants that specialize in seafood. Add skeletons using the MUSIC and CON-TACTS databases. Print the screen showing the addition of skeletons. Remove the MUSIC and CONTACTS databases.

Create a query where CUISINE equals Seafood. Add the MUSIC and CONTACTS databases as skeletons. Print the screen. Remove the MUSIC and CONTACTS database skeletons and save the query as Seafood. Print the query.

6

Creating Complex Queries

The exact-match query searches described in the preceding chapter have limited use. Locating every record in a car dealership database for which the selling price of the vehicle was exactly $12,500 or the delivery date was 2/14/92 may not be as meaningful as finding out how many vehicles sold for more than $12,500 during the last quarter. dBASE IV provides a number of query-based alternatives to exact-match, one-condition searches.

Using the relational operators > (greater than), < (less than), and = (equal to), you can greatly extend your power to search for records. Combining these operators gives you additional flexibility to find data in your database.

A set of special operators, $ (Contains), Like, and Sounds Like$, facilitates finding records using vague criteria. You can use the $ operator to find a specific character string hidden inside a longer character string in a field, for example. The Like operator conducts wild-card searches that enable you to find several variations of a spelling. The Sounds Like operator enables you to search a database using phonetic approximations of actual data.

A group of summary operators enables you to count, average, or sum the contents of numeric fields of all records or records that meet specified criteria. Two other summary operators permit you to select the one record from a group of records that contains the highest (MAX) or lowest (MIN) value in a given field.

You can establish AND and OR relationships to help find records that meet multiple conditions, fall within a range, or meet one of several possible conditions.

The techniques described in this chapter offer a highly sophisticated toolbox of methods for selecting very precise groups of information from a database. A word of caution is in order, however. Writing queries can be far more complex than the examples in this book. As you learn to use more complex queries, follow one golden rule: test your query before you use it on the actual database. Make a small test database; you can extract the records from the larger database. Do not include more records in the test database than you can reasonably look at to verify the results of your queries. Before you run a query, identify all records that should be acted on by the query in the test database. If the query finds every record you are looking for without extra records, then you can run your query on the real database with confidence.

Objectives

1. To Work with Relational Operators
2. To Work with Special Operators
3. To Work with AND and OR Conditions
4. To Use Summary Operators

150

Key Terms Used in This Chapter	
File skeleton	The upper portion of the Query Design work surface in which the user must specify the field contents used to select records in a query operation.
Calculated fields	The left area in the middle portion of the Query Design work surface in which the user can define one or more fields that are not part of the database.
Condition box	The right area in the middle portion of the Query Design work surface in which the user can specify complex conditions involving several fields.
View skeleton	The lower portion of the Query Design work surface in which the user must specify the fields to display (on-screen or to the printer) from the records selected.
Operator	A symbol used in a query to select a record based on a variety of data matches or numeric conditions. An operator shows the relationship between data and search criteria.

7

Objective 1: To Work with Relational Operators

You are not limited to searches in which you place a criterion in the file skeleton and find only those records containing an exact match. By using one of the relational operators or operator combinations, your searches can be more flexible. Several relational operators might be familiar to you.

Basic relational operators are as follows:

=	Equal to
>	Greater than
<	Less than

151

Relational operator combinations are as follows:

>=	Greater than or equal to
<=	Less than or equal to
<> or #	Not equal to

Using the equal (=) operator has the same effect as using no operator. You can type either "**Fox**" or ="**Fox**" as the search condition under a file skeleton field name and produce the same result.

Keep in mind the following rules for entering the most common search conditions:

Field type	Search condition format
Character	Enclose the condition in quotation marks
Numeric	Enter the value without quotation marks
Date	Enclose the date in braces { }

Using a Single Relational Operator

When you type a search condition without an operator, you are requesting an = (equal to) search.

Use > (greater than) to find all records in which a value exceeds the stated number, a date falls after the stated date, or a character field entry starts with a letter that appears after the stated letter in the alphabet.

Use < (less than) to find all records in which a value is less than the stated number, a date falls before the stated date, or a character field entry starts with a letter that appears after the stated letter in the alphabet.

Exercise 1.1: Working with a Single Relational Operator

To create a query containing a single relational operator and view the results in Browse mode, follow these steps:.

1. Access the dBASE IV Control Center and then access the CARS database.

2. Highlight the desired database name in the Data panel, press ⏎Enter, and then select Use file.

3. Highlight Create in the Queries panel and then press ⏎Enter.

4. Enter >{01/01/92}, the condition to restrict record selection that is preceded by a relational operator, under the search field name DATE_DEL in the file skeleton in the upper portion of the Query Design work surface (see fig. 7.1). This search condition specifies all records in which delivery date is after January 1, 1992.

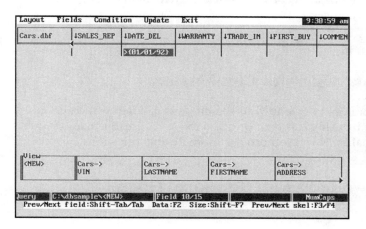

Fig. 7.1
The search condition that specifies a delivery date after January 1, 1992.

5. Set up the query-controlled display of fields in the view skeleton in the lower portion of the Query Design work surface (see Chapter 6).

6. Press F2 to see the results in Browse mode or Edit mode (press F2 again if Edit mode appears rather than Browse mode).

Variations of single operator search conditions are illustrated in the following examples:

Condition	Records Found
>"F"	Finds all records in which the character field entry begins with G through Z
<"F"	Finds all records in which the character field entry begins with A through E

continues

continued

Condition	Records Found
>24000	Finds all records in which the numeric field entry is greater than 24000
<24000	Finds all records in which the numeric field entry is less than 24000
<{01,01,92}	Finds all records in which the date field entry is before January 1, 1992

Using Relational Operator Combinations

Combine query operators to extend your search power. When you combine relational operators by using less than or equal to (<=), greater than or equal to (>=), or not equal to (<>), you can ask more flexible questions.

Exercise 1.2: Working with Relational Operator Combinations

To create a query containing an equal sign combination and view the results in Browse mode, follow these steps:

1. Access the Query Design work surface (open a database and select Create in the Queries panel), and then set up the desired view skeleton in the lower portion of the screen.

2. Enter the condition to restrict record selection (preceded by the desired equal sign combination) under the search field name in the file skeleton in the upper portion of the screen (see fig. 7.2). This search condition specifies all records in which delivery date is on or before January 15, 1992.

3. Press F2 to see the results in Browse mode or Edit mode.

If you don't combine operators, you have to specify a search condition as <{01/16/92} to see all records on or before 01/15/92. Now you can write <={01/15/92}, which is easier to read and understand at a glance.

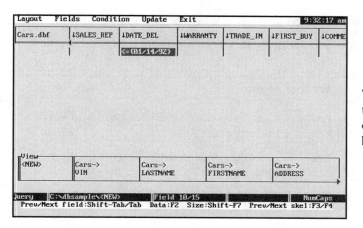

Fig. 7.2
The search condition that specifies a delivery date on or before January 15, 1992.

Exercise 1.3: Negating Relational Operators

To set up a query that excludes selected records, follow these steps:

1. Access the Query Design work surface (open a database and select Create in the Queries panel), and then set up the desired view skeleton in the lower portion of the screen.

2. Enter the condition #"Weist" to restrict record selection (preceded by the not equal to operator) under the search field name in the file skeleton at the top of the Query Design work surface (see fig. 7.3).

   Entering #"Weist" serves the same purpose as entering <> "Weist"; the search condition selects all records except those in which the last name is Weist.

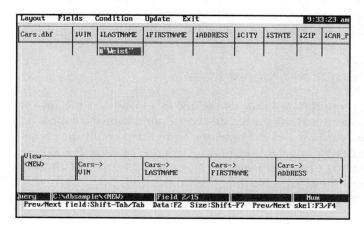

Fig. 7.3
The search condition that excludes the last name Weist.

3. Press ⬚F2⬚ to see the results in Browse mode or Edit mode.

Variations of operator combination search conditions are illustrated in the following examples:

Condition	Records Found
>="F"	Finds all records in which the character field entry begins with F through Z
<="F"	Finds all records in which the character field entry begins with A through F
>=24000	Finds all records in which the numeric field entry is greater than or equal to 24000
<=24000	Finds all records in which the numeric field entry is less than or equal to 24000
<={12,31,91}	Finds all records in which the date field entry is before January 1, 1992

Objective 2: To Work with Special Operators

Three special operators—Contains ($), Like, and Sounds Like—make your searches even more flexible and versatile. Many searches go beyond merely determining a relationship. You may need to find a set of characters embedded in a larger character string, locate every address on a particular street, or find a name that sounds like, but is not spelled like, another word.

Using the Contains ($) Operator

Character fields often contain key words embedded in a manner that is difficult to search. If you were to look for records concerning lamps in a furniture store's inventory database, for example, the word *lamp* could appear anywhere within the description field (beginning, middle, or end). If you type a search criterion with the Contains operator ($), such as $"lamp", dBASE IV finds *Floor lamp*, *brass lamp*, *hanging lamp*, and *lamp table*.

In earlier illustrations of query character field search conditions, text typed between quotation marks has been an exact match to database contents, including case. You can conduct a search that isn't case-sensitive by using the Queries panel and creating a calculated field that includes the UPPER( ) function previously discussed in Chapter 5.

Exercise 2.1: Working with the Contains Operator

To include the Contains ($) operator in a case-sensitive query search and view the results in Browse mode, follow these steps:

1. Access the Query Design work surface and then set up the desired view skeleton.

2. Enter the Contains ($) operator and the condition to restrict record selection, $"RS", under the search field name in the file skeleton (see fig. 7.4).

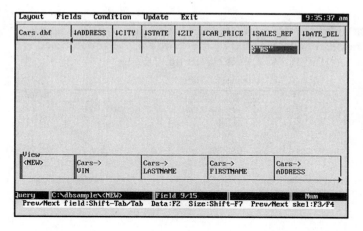

Fig. 7.4
The search condition that restricts record selection.

3. Press F2 to see the results in Browse mode or Edit mode.

Exercise 2.2: Creating a Calculated Field Skeleton

To write a search criterion that is not case-sensitive, create a calculated fields skeleton that uses the UPPER( ) function. Then follow these steps:

1. Access the Query Design work surface and then set up the desired view skeleton.

157

2. Press ⟨Alt⟩+ ⟨F⟩ to select the Fields menu.

3. Press ⟨C⟩ to select Create Calculated Field (see fig. 7.5).

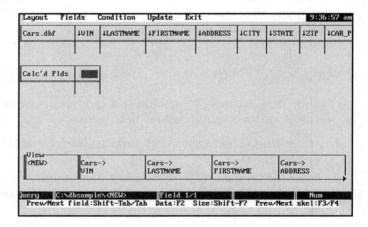

Fig. 7.5
A Calc'd Flds box appears in the center of the work surface.

4. In the highlighted box in the calculated fields skeleton, type the name of the field to be searched preceded by the word *UPPER* and encased in parentheses ( ) **UPPER(SALES_REP)**(see fig. 7.6).

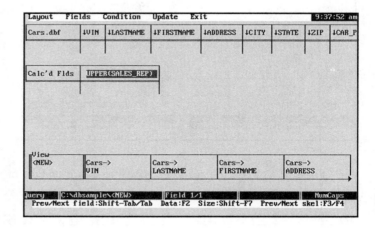

Fig. 7.6
The field name entered in the Calculated field box.

As an alternative, press ⟨Shift⟩+ ⟨F1⟩ to select the appropriate option from the function column—in this case, UPPER( )—and insert the field name into the parentheses.

5. Beneath the field name in the calculated fields skeleton, enter the search criterion (see fig. 7.7).

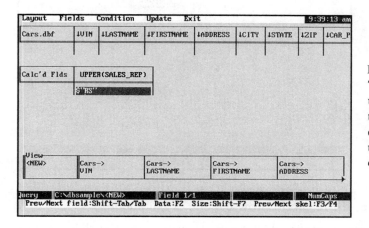

Fig. 7.7
The condition using UPPER() that selects records containing upper- or lower-case characters.

6. Press F2 to see the results in Browse mode or Edit mode.

Using the Like Operator

Wild cards work in the Queries panel in the same manner they work in the Data panel. The * symbol replaces a group of characters in a search criterion string, and the ? symbol replaces a single character. You must type the operator Like first, however.

Exercise 2.3: Working with the Like Operator

To create a search for records when you are unsure of the correct spelling or want to see a group of similar records, follow these steps:

1. Access the Query Design work surface and set up the desired view skeleton.

2. Enter the Like search condition Like "*Ca?e *" in the search field of the file skeleton (see fig. 7.8). Entering this condition locates the records of all customers who live on streets such as *Cape*, *Cate*, or *Cake*.

7

159

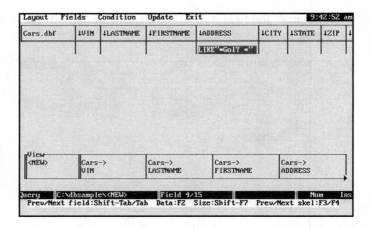

Fig. 7.8
The Like search
condition.

3. Press F2 to see the results in Browse mode or Edit mode.

All records with a street name in which the first, second, and fourth letters are *C*, *a*, and *e*, respectively, have been selected.

To perform a search that is not case-sensitive, enter the Like search condition in the calculated fields skeleton using the UPPER( ) function rather than entering the search condition in the file skeleton in the upper portion of the screen.

Using the Sounds Like Operator

If you have experienced a situation in which you vaguely remember a name but not the spelling, you can appreciate the Sounds Like operator. In setting up most of your query search conditions, you know how to spell at least part of the desired field contents. One of dBASE IV's new features, Soundex, enables you to find field contents based on a *sounds like* search condition. In other words, you can use a version of the Like operator, Sounds Like, to guess at the spelling in a field.

Exercise 2.4: Working with the Sounds Like Feature

To use the Sounds Like feature, enter phonetic or abbreviated spelling in the search condition. Follow these steps:

1. Access the Query Design work surface and set up the desired view skeleton.

160

2. Enter the search criterion preceded by the operator Sounds Like (see fig. 7.9). To search for the first name Kasey when the exact spelling is unknown, enter the phonetic criterion Sounds Like "KC".

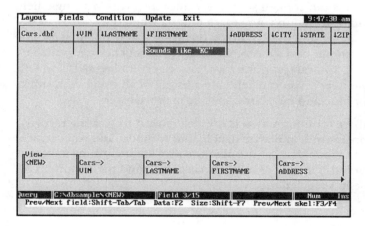

Fig. 7.9
A search criterion with the Sounds Like operator.

3. Press [F2] to see the results in Browse mode. The abbreviated search condition KC finds a record in which the first name is Kasey.

Using Sounds Like requires trial-and-error. If you type the search condition Sounds Like Casey or Sounds Like Casee, for example, dBASE IV does not find a record containing Kasey. If you type the search condition **Sounds Like KC** or **Sounds Like Ksee**, however, dBASE IV can find a record containing Kasey.

Objective 3: To Work with AND and OR Conditions

Up to this point, queries have illustrated searching on the contents of a single field using relational operators (variations of =, >, <) and special operators ($ [Contains], Like, and Sounds Like) in a single search condition. The information you need may be more complex than merely looking for data in a single field, however.

Query search conditions can span several fields. Use AND logic in setting up your search criteria when all conditions must be met for dBASE IV to find a record. Suppose that salesman Roger Stone wants a follow-up contact list of all his customers who bought a car more than two years ago. To compile the

161

list, he can find all records in a car sales database in which the salesman is RS (Roger Stone) in the SALES_REP field and the date of delivery is more than two years ago.

Query search conditions can contain several specifications within a single field (OR logic). Use OR logic to set up your search criteria when only one search condition must be met for dBASE IV to find a record. If you maintain a furniture inventory, for example, and a customer asks which couches are available in either of two colors, you can produce a list. You can combine AND and OR conditions in a single query. You can generate a listing of all couches in stock that are either red or blue and made by a specific manufacturer.

Querying your database for information is not just limited to locating records. Several arithmetic operators summarize data in Query mode, and you can see the results in the Data mode. Summary operators provide the means to sum, average, or count records meeting search criteria and to find the minimum or maximum field value in specified records.

Using AND Conditions

If you specify AND search conditions, two (or more) criteria must be met before the record is selected. AND relationships can be specified between different fields or in the same field.

To specify an AND relationship between fields, enter the search criteria on the same line beneath field names in the file skeleton.

Exercise 3.1: Using the AND Condition

To use the AND condition, follow these steps:

1. Access the Query Design work surface and set up the desired view skeleton.
2. Enter the first search condition "C" beneath the field name in the file skeleton (see fig. 7.10). The criterion indicates that a record will be selected only if the MEM_TYPE field contains the code *C* for corporate members.
3. Enter the second search condition "History" beneath a field name on the same line as the first search condition (see fig. 7.11). This criterion indicates that a record will be selected only if the SIG field entry contains the word History.

162

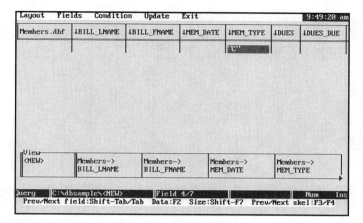

Fig. 7.10
The first search
condition.

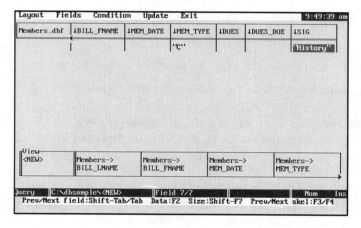

Fig. 7.11
The second search
condition.

4. Press F2 to see the results in Browse mode or Edit mode (see fig. 7.12).

If you continue to enter AND search conditions on the same line in the file skeleton, dBASE IV treats these fields as an AND relationship and selects records only if all criteria are true.

You also can establish an AND relationship in the same field to select a range of records. Enter the search conditions beneath the single field name, separated by a comma.

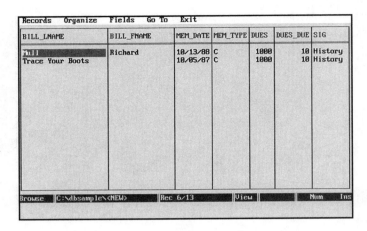

Fig. 7.12
The Browse mode display limited to records meeting both search conditions "C" and "History".

Exercise 3.2: Using the AND Condition in the Same Field

To use the AND condition to find records in the same file, follow these steps:

1. Access the Query Design work surface and set up the desired view skeleton.

2. Enter the search criteria >=4,<=6 in a single column (see fig. 7.13). This range criteria beneath the DUES_DUE field name specifies all records in which dues are due in months 4, 5, and 6 (April, May, and June).

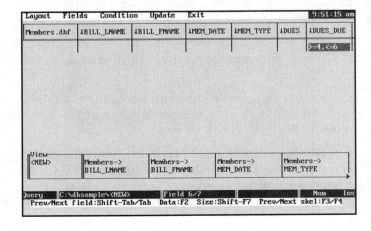

Fig. 7.13
A range criteria.

3. Press F2 to see the results in Browse mode or Edit mode.

Using OR Conditions

OR conditions, like AND conditions, can have relationships between fields as well as in a field. Use OR conditions to choose from a series of conditions. Only one condition must be true, however, to cause the record to be selected.

To enter OR conditions based on the contents of a single field, enter the criteria on separate lines in the column headed by the appropriate field name.

Exercise 3.3: Working with the OR Condition

To use the OR condition to find the records of one field, follow these steps:

1. Access the Query Design work surface and set up the desired view skeleton.

2. Enter OR conditions on separate lines beneath the search field in the file skeleton (see fig. 7.14). To choose a record whose MEM_TYPE is either S or F, type "S", press ⬇, and type "F".

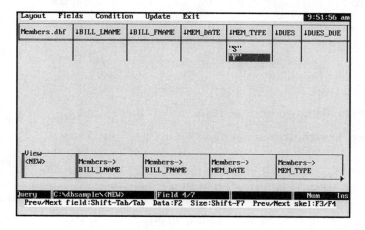

Fig. 7.14
Two OR conditions in the same search field.

3. Press F2 to see the results in Browse mode or Edit mode (see fig. 7.15).

Note that each OR condition is entered in the same field but on different lines. Entering conditions on different lines tells dBASE IV that the conditions are in an OR relationship.

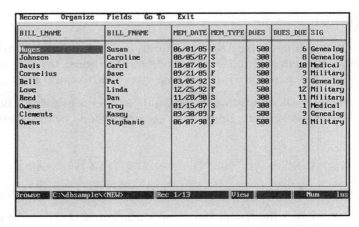

Fig. 7.15
The Browse mode
display limited to
records containing
F or S in the
MEM_TYPE field.

BILL_LNAME	BILL_FNAME	MEM_DATE	MEM_TYPE	DUES	DUES_DUE	SIG
Huges	Susan	06/01/85	F	500	6	Genealog
Johnson	Caroline	08/05/87	S	300	8	Genealog
Davis	Carol	10/07/86	S	300	10	Medical
Cornelius	Dave	09/21/85	F	500	9	Military
Bell	Pat	03/05/92	S	300	3	Genealog
Love	Linda	12/25/92	F	500	12	Military
Reed	Dan	11/28/90	S	300	11	Military
Owens	Troy	01/15/87	S	300	1	Medical
Clements	Kasey	09/30/89	F	500	9	Genealog
Owens	Stephanie	06/07/90	F	500	6	Military

You also can specify OR conditions based on entries in two or more fields.
Enter the first OR condition on the first line beneath the first search field,
enter the second OR condition on the second line beneath the next search
field, and continue to drop to the next line to specify each additional OR
condition.

Exercise 3.4: Entering Conditions Using Two or More Fields

To use the OR condition with two or more fields, follow these steps:

1. Access the Query Design work surface and set up the desired view
   skeleton.

2. Using ⟨Tab⟩ and ⟨Shift⟩+⟨Tab⟩, position the highlight below the first
   search field name MEM_TYPE in the file skeleton, and enter the search
   condition "S".

3. Using ⟨Tab⟩ and ⟨Shift⟩+⟨Tab⟩, position the highlight below the
   second field name SIG, press ↓ to move the highlight down one line,
   and enter the next criterion "Genealogy" (see fig. 7.16).

4. Press ⟨F2⟩ to see the results in Browse mode or Edit mode.

Caution: Although you can mix AND and OR conditions in a query, be sure to
test such a query to verify that the results are accurate and serve the intended
purpose of the search.

166

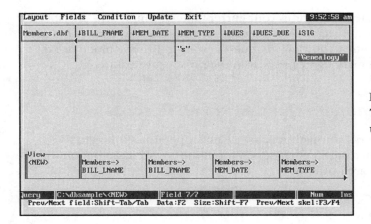

Fig. 7.16
The OR condition
used in two fields.

Objective 4: To Use Summary Operators

dBASE IV lets you summarize the values in some fields, gaining information without writing custom programs. You need only apply your choice of operators to all records in the database or to selected records in the database. The following table provides information about the summary operators.

Operator	Use on Data Types	Explanation
AVERAGE or AVG	Float/Numeric	Averages the contents of the specified field
COUNT or CNT	Character/Date/Float /Numeric/Logical	Counts the number of records that meet the query criteria. If no search criteria are specified, all records are counted.
MAX	Character/Date /Float/Numeric	Finds the highest or maximum value of a group of records
MIN	Character/Date /Float/Numeric	Finds the lowest or minimum value of a group of records
SUM	Float/Numeric	Totals the contents of the specified field for a group of records

167

To include a summary operator in your current query, simply type the specific operator under the applicable field name in the file skeleton. You do not see individual records when you view the query results in Browse mode or Edit mode; instead, summary figures appear in their respective columns.

Applying a Summary Operator to All Records

To generate summary information using a single operator applied to the entire database, enter the summary operator in the file skeleton but omit specification of a search condition.

Exercise 4.1: Using the AVG or AVERAGE Summary Operator

Follow these steps to average a numeric field's contents for all records in a database:

1. Access the Query Design work surface and set up the desired view skeleton.
2. Use Tab↔ and ⇧Shift + Tab↔ to position the highlight below the first search field name CAR_PRICE in the file skeleton.
3. Enter the summary operator AVERAGE or AVG (see fig. 7.17). This operator generates the average selling price in the database.

Fig. 7.17
The AVERAGE operator generates the average selling price in a vehicle sales database.

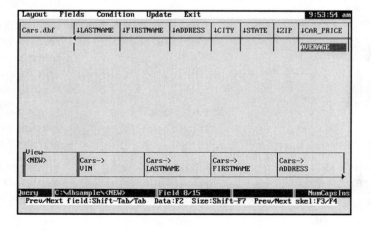

4. Press F2 to see the results in Browse mode or Edit mode (see fig. 7.18). Records do not appear on the Browse screen.

168

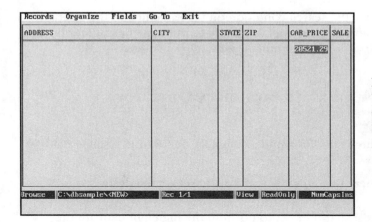

Fig. 7.18
The Browse mode
display of the
average price paid
for a car.

To further illustrate the use of a summary operator without record restrictions, determine the latest date in a date field using the MAX summary operator.

Exercise 4.2: Using the MAX Summary Operator

To use the MAX summary operator, follow these steps:

1. Access the Query Design work surface and set up the desired view skeleton.

2. Use `Tab↕` and `⇧Shift` + `Tab↕` to position the highlight beneath the appropriate field name heading in the file skeleton.

3. Enter the **MAX** operator beneath the DATE_DEL field heading to determine the most recent date a vehicle was delivered.

4. Press `F2` to see the results in Browse mode or Edit mode.

You also can substitute COUNT to tally the total number of records in the database, SUM to add the contents of a float or numeric field, or MIN to return the lowest (or oldest) value.

Applying a Summary Operator to Limited Records

Only one summary operator can appear in one field at a time, although several operators may appear in different fields in a query. If you apply a summary operator to a limited number of records rather than all the records

169

in the database, enter the search condition on the same line as the operator. If the search condition and the operator apply to the same field, enter both conditions in the appropriate column, separated by a comma.

Exercise 4.3: Applying a Summary Operator to a Single Field

To enter both a search condition and a summary operator in a single field, follow these steps:

1. Access the Query Design work surface and set up the desired view skeleton.

2. Use Tab⇄ and ⇧Shift + Tab⇄ to position the highlight beneath the WARRANTY field name in the file skeleton.

3. Enter the summary operator COUNT and the search criterion .F. (false) in the same column, separated by a comma (see fig. 7.19).

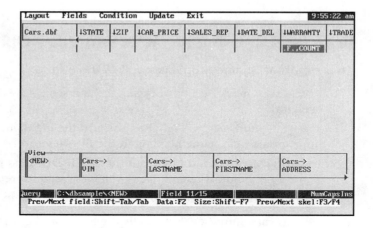

Fig. 7.19
The summary operator COUNT and the search criterion .F. in the same column.

4. Press F2 to see the results in Browse mode or Edit mode.

Exercise 4.4: Applying a Summary Operator to Different Fields

To enter a search condition and a summary operator that apply to different fields, follow these steps:

1. Access the Query Design work surface and set up the desired view skeleton.

2. Use `Tab⇅` and `⇧Shift` + `Tab⇅` to position the highlight beneath the SALES_REP field name in the file skeleton and enter the search condition "SAM".

3. Use `Tab⇅` and `⇧Shift` + `Tab⇅` to position the highlight beneath the field name DATE_DEL in the file skeleton and enter the summary operator MAX.

4. Press `F2` to see the results, the most recent delivery date for a car sold by the specified salesperson, in Browse mode or Edit mode

You can combine any of the summary operators (COUNT, AVERAGE, SUM, MAX, and MIN) with one or more search conditions as long as you do not enter more than one summary operator in a single column in the file skeleton. As your queries become more complex, remember to test your query results for accuracy.

Chapter Summary

In this chapter, you learned to create queries which select records based on a search condition other than a simple exact match. The next chapter presents the Forms panel for designing custom screens.

Testing Your Knowledge

True/False Questions

1. By typing a search condition without an operator, you are requesting an = (equal to) search.

2. Combining query operators limits your search power.

3. You can combine AND and OR conditions in a single query.

4. Using OR conditions requires both conditions to be true.

5. Only one summary operator can appear in one field at a time, although several operators may appear in different fields in a query.

171

Multiple Choice Questions

1. Use the > (greater than) relational operator to find all records
   A. equal to the field entry.
   B. greater than or equal to the field entry.
   C. greater than the stated value, stated date, and stated character field.
   D. greater than the numeric value 0 and character field space.
   E. greater than the numeric values only.

2. To find all records less than or equal to SAM, you would type in the search field name
   A. =<SAM
   B. <=SAM
   C. <"SAM"
   D. ="SAM"
   E. <="SAM"

3. Three special operators that make searches even more flexible and versatile are
   A. #, Line, and Sounds Like.
   B. $, Like, and Sounds Like.
   C. $, Equal, and Sounds Like.
   D. >, =, and <.
   E. $, Sounds, and Like.

4. If you enter search conditions for two fields on the same line, you are using the
   A. OR condition.
   B. AND condition.
   C. NOT condition.
   D. ELSE condition.
   E. NULL condition.

5. Which of the following summary operators counts the number of records that meet the query criteria?
   A. AVG or AVERAGE
   B. MAX
   C. MIN
   D. SUM
   E. COUNT or CNT

7

Fill-in-the-Blank Questions

1. Use _____ to find all records in which a value is less than the stated number.

2. The _____ symbol replaces a group of characters in a search criterion string, and the _____ symbol replaces a single character.

3. Use _____ logic to set up your search criteria when only one search condition must be met for dBASE IV to find a record.

4. To generate summary information using a single operator applied to the entire database, enter the _____ operator in the file skeleton but omit specification of a _____ condition.

5. You can substitute _____ to tally the total number of records in the database, _____ to add the contents of a float or numeric field, or _____ to return the lowest (or oldest) value.

Review: Short Projects

1. Creating a Query

   Select the Inventory catalog and access the PRODUCT database from Chapter 3. Create a query that will find all product codes greater than one of the codes in the data base. Print a quick report of the PRODUCT database and then print the screen of the query.

2. Using AND in a Query

   Select Inventory catalog and access the EQUIPMENT database. Create a query that will find records that have the same type field and date purchased field. Remember that both criteria must be true. Use the AND condition. Save the query as Type.

3. Using MAX, SUM, and MIN in a Query

   Select Inventory catalog and access the EQUIPMENT database. Create a query, and include summary operators in the following fields: use MAX to find the oldest age of equipment, SUM to find price of the equipment, and MIN to find the earliest date of purchase.

7

Review: Long Projects

1. Creating and Printing Queries

   Select the Business catalog and select the database MUSIC. Create a query to find all records with prices higher than $13.95. Create a query to find all records in which Type is equal to CD and Category is equal to ROCK. Be sure to save each query. Use Quick report to print each query.

2. Creating and Printing Queries

   Select the Business catalog and select the database RESTAURANT. Create a query to find all records with same location and cuisine. Save the query as Target. Create another query to count the restaurants by using the summary operator; use CNT for the number of restaurants. Save the query as Count. Use Quick report to print each query.

7

Designing
Custom
Screens

From the Forms panel on the Control Center, you can design and create your own custom screens and benefit from a number of advantages over using the dBASE IV Browse or Edit screen displays. You can design a custom screen to display selected fields in a different order than the fields appear in the database, for example. You also can add text to the screen to make the display more informative, such as entering the title of the database in use.

Perhaps the most common use of the Forms panel involves creating data-entry screens that look like the paper forms (*source documents*) on which data is initially recorded. When the screen and a source document are similar, you can enter data with greater speed.

If you choose to create a custom screen, you can establish your own contents for the navigation and message lines. You can have the message Enter the two-digit state code in uppercase to appear whenever the cursor rests on a state field, for example. You also can improve the accuracy of data entry by including editing criteria in the custom form. You can specify that the only acceptable initials to enter in a sales representative field are ABC, XYZ, or LCM. dBASE then prevents entry of any other combination of upper- or lowercase letters.

Objectives

1. To Use the Forms Design Screen
2. To Create a Custom Screen
3. To Modify and Enhance the Layout of a Custom Screen
4. To Use Templates and Picture Functions
5. To Use Edit Options To Control Data Entry
6. To Use the Custom Form

8

Key Terms Used in This Chapter	
Custom screen	A screen you design for data entry or information display, as compared to the standard Browse or Edit screen provided by dBASE IV.
Editor	The limited dBASE IV word-processor. You can use it in a variety of settings, including creating a custom screen or entering narrative into a memo field.
Layout mode	The Editor's mode when you access the Forms panel to design custom forms.
Template	A pattern of editing characters that controls what type of data can be entered in each character position in a field (for example, first character an uppercase letter of the alphabet, second character a number, and so forth).
Picture function	An editing feature similar to a template except that a picture function applies to an entire field (for example, all uppercase).
Edit options	Features that can be used with any field on a custom form to limit allowable data to specific entries or a range of entries (for example, entries in a month field must be in the range 1 to 12).

Objective 1: To Use the Forms Design Screen

As you become familiar with the many dBASE IV features, you can see some similarities among various screens. The upper portion of the Forms screen displays a menu bar like the Data and Queries screens, for example. A status bar, navigation line, and message line appear in the lower portion of the screen, with the remaining area referred to as the Forms Design work surface.

Understanding the Work Surface

The Data Design work surfaces—for creating a file structure or entering data in Browse mode or Edit mode—follow a standard format. When you create a file structure, for example, you must supply the name, type, width, and decimal information for each field as prompted on-screen. The work surface for adding or editing records also is clearly defined: one record on each screen in Edit mode, and records in row-and-column format in Browse mode. The Query work surface too is structured to control how it is used, with the file skeleton across the upper portion and the view skeleton in the lower portion.

The Forms Design work surface is less structured than either the Data Design work surface or the Query Design work surface. You create a form on this work surface much as you might take a clean piece of paper and start drawing a design. Think of the work surface (also called the Editor) as your paper. Your tools are the options in the menu bar, the information items in the status bar, and the keyboard combinations and instructions described in the navigation and message lines.

Exercise 1.1: Accessing the Forms Design Work Surface

To access a blank Forms Design work surface, follow these steps:

1. Access the dBASE IV Control Center.
2. Highlight the Create option at the top of the Forms panel and press ⏎Enter. When you create a form without a database (file) or query (view) active, the work surface appears with the Layout pull-down menu displayed (see fig. 8.1).

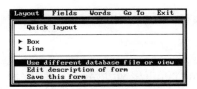

Fig. 8.1
The Layout pull-
down menu.

3. Press U to select Use Different Database File or View. A picklist appears in the upper right corner of the screen, displaying a list of all databases and view files.

4. Press ↑ and ↓ to highlight the name of the database or view file you intend to use and press ↵Enter. A blank Forms Design work surface appears (see fig. 8.2).

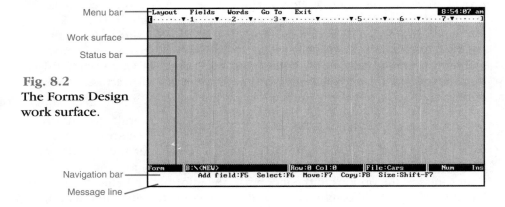

Menu bar

Work surface

Status bar

Fig. 8.2
The Forms Design
work surface.

Navigation bar

Message line

The limited dBASE IV word processor called the Editor is active in Form mode. You already are familiar with the Editor; the work surface is the same one you use to enter the contents of Memo fields (see Chapter 3). The Editor has two modes, Word Wrap and Layout, depending on which dBASE IV feature you are using.

When you access the Data panel and enter comments in a Memo field, you use the Editor in Word-Wrap mode. Word-Wrap mode works like a word processor and is ideally suited for entering continuous text.

When you access the Forms panel, the Editor is in Layout mode. Layout mode, a large highlighted area between the menu bar and the status bar, appears as a blank screen often referred to as a *blackboard*. Layout mode is ideally suited for designing forms; you can type anywhere on it. You can type text on this surface, add data field templates, draw boxes and lines, and move or copy

178

portions of the screen. Each line is separate from others—the text does not wrap.

As you use more complex databases, your forms may become too large to fit on one screen. Making multiple-screen forms is easy. When you exceed the capacity of one screen, the Editor creates a second screen like the second page of a two-page form.

Using the Status Bar

The status bar is divided into five sections (see fig. 8.3). Each section displays information designed to keep you informed of the status of the current form. If you have not named the form, the word New is displayed.

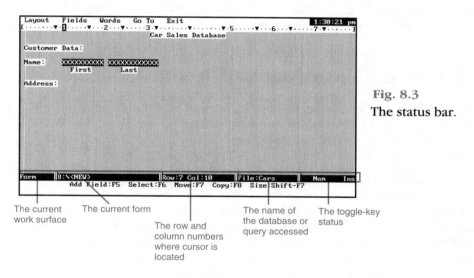

Fig. 8.3
The status bar.

8

The current work surface

The current form

The row and column numbers where cursor is located

The name of the database or query accessed

The toggle-key status

Using the Navigation and Message Lines

You should look at the navigation line to stay informed about what keys are active at the moment (see fig. 8.4). These keys change while you are copying and moving items on the work surface.

The navigation line in figure 8.4 indicates that you can press [F5] to see a list of fields and then select a field to transfer to the work surface. Press [F6] to highlight a rectangle on the work surface. The highlighted rectangle can be deleted, moved, or copied. Press [F7] to move the highlighted rectangle to another location on the work surface. Press [F8] to copy the highlighted rectangle. Press [⇧Shift]+[F7] to increase or decrease the size of a window box or template.

179

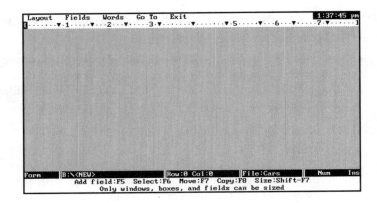

Fig. 8.4
The navigation
line.

Watch the message line for important instructions when you are moving,
copying, or sizing items on the work surface.

Objective 2: To Create a Custom Screen

You should have a clear design in mind before you start creating a custom
form. If only selected fields from a database will appear on the form or if you
want to rearrange the order and placement of many fields, start the creation
process from a blank screen and individually select each field.

As an alternative, use the Quick Layout option (discussed in a later section in
this chapter) on the Layout menu if you want all or most of the database fields
to display on your custom screen in the order in which they appear in the
database structure. Whichever method you choose, you can perform the same
activities: add, delete, and rearrange fields following instructions in the
navigation and message lines; add additional descriptive text; enhance form
appearance with boxes and lines; and save the custom form.

Designing the Custom Screen

Before you create a custom form, sketch the layout of the screen or screens on
paper (see fig. 8.5). You can speed up preliminary design work by laying out
proposed screens in a word processing program. The dimensions of each
screen should be no larger than 80 characters wide by 21 lines long. Although
you can move fields and text around on the Forms Design work surface, you
can save time by entering a well-thought-out design. After you create rough
sketches of your fields and text, check your ideas with anyone else who might
use or approve the custom form.

180

```
┌─────────────────────────────────────────────────────────┐
│                    New Car Sales                          │
│Customer name: xxxxxxxxxx xxxxxxxxxxxx   Date of Delivery: mm/dd/yy   │
│              (first)    (last)      Vehicle ID Number: xxxxxxxxxx    │
│                                                           │
│Address: xxxxxxxxxxxxxxxxxxxxxxxxx                         │
│City: xxxxxxxxxxxxxxx State: xx                            │
│Zip: xxxxx   Phone: (999)999-9999                         │
│                                                           │
│Car Price: 99,999.99                  Sales Representative: xxx │
│-----------------------------------------------------------│
│ /------------------\     Warranty  : Y/N                  │
│ | Buyer Attributes |     Trade-in  : Y/N                  │
│ \------------------/     First-time : Y/N                 │
│                                                           │
│Comments: xxxxxxxxxxxxxxxxxxxxxxx 150 characters xxxxxxxxxxxxxxxxxxxxxxxxxxx │
└─────────────────────────────────────────────────────────┘
```

Fig. 8.5
The proposed layout.

The layout shown in figure 8.5 is designed very close to scale. The spacing indicated by *XXX* and *999* takes into account field sizes specified in the database structure. Descriptive field names are not limited to the actual field names defined in the database structure.

When designing a form, use only lines 1 through 21 on each screen. dBASE IV uses lines 0, 22, 23, and 24 to display the menu bar, status bar, navigation line, and message line. Also, do not use double quotation marks (") on-screen; dBASE IV beeps to indicate the error but does not specify the nature of it. As you develop a custom form, periodically check your work by pressing F2 (Data) to see what the screen looks like as a data-entry form. F2 activates Browse mode or Edit mode. Return to the Design work surface by using ⇧Shift + F2 (Design).

Adding Descriptive Text

Each custom form you design generally contains descriptive text as well as fields. The text can include a title at the top of the form and expanded names for each field. Although you can use the field names from the database structure, dBASE IV's 10-character field-name limit may make interpreting some field names difficult; the descriptive text does not have that character limitation. If you have VIN as a field, for example, consider entering the text *Vehicle Identification Number* to help the user understand the field contents to follow.

You may prefer to enter all the form's descriptive text first, leaving space for a field template beside each descriptive field name. A field template appears as a series of XXXX's (character field), a series of 9999's (numeric or float field), MM/DD/YY (date field), or L (logical field). The space occupied by a field template corresponds with the field width specified in the file structure.

8

Use ←, →, ↑, or ↓ to position the cursor and then type your text, editing with •Backspace and Del. Remember that word wrap is not active. Refer to your rough sketches of the screen layout to make sure that you have included all your fields. Periodically press F2 (Data) to see what the actual form looks like. When you are satisfied with the initial text design, you can add the field templates.

Exercise 2.1: Entering Descriptive Text

To begin creating a custom form by entering all the descriptive text first (leaving space for each field template), follow these steps:

1. Access the dBASE IV Control Center, highlight the Create option in the upper portion of the Forms panel and then press ↵Enter.

2. Press U to select Use Different Database File or View, highlight the CARS database and press ↵Enter.

3. Position the cursor at the location where the first text should begin and type the form title New Car Sales in the upper portion of the Forms Design screen (see fig. 8.6).

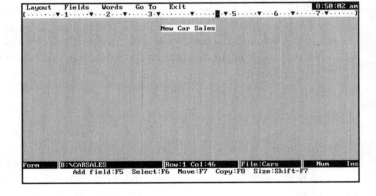

Fig. 8.6
Begin by adding a form title at the top of the Forms Design screen.

4. Add the descriptive field names shown in figure 8.7. At this point, you are typing field descriptions. The actual field templates will be added later. Frequently compare your custom form design with the custom screen layout being created on the Forms Design work surface.

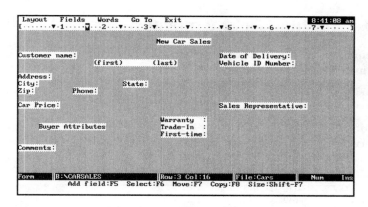

Fig. 8.7
The custom screen layout being created on the Forms Design work surface.

5. Press [F2] to preview how your form is progressing. dBASE IV takes a few seconds to generate a custom form. Information about form generation appears on the message line and in the status bar.

6. Press [⇧Shift]+[F2] to return to the Forms Design work surface.

Adding Fields

To specify inclusion of a field in a custom form, position the cursor on the Forms Design work surface where you want the field to start and press [F5]. After you select your choice of a field name from a picklist of field names, the corresponding default field template appears on the form.

A field template is a pattern of editing characters that controls what type of data can be entered in each character position in a field. The template XXXXXX indicates that up to six characters (alphabetic or numeric) may appear in the field, for example. The template 9999 restricts entry to a maximum of four numbers; the template MM/DD/YY accepts only dates.

Field templates transferred to the Forms Design work surface using by [F5] have the same type and width characteristics as the field definitions set up in the database structure. In a later section, you learn to edit the template defaults.

Generally, templates are placed to the right of the field name. They can be placed above or below the associated descriptive text, according to your design sketch, however.

8

183

Exercise 2.2: Establishing Field Templates

To establish field templates on the Forms Design work surface without altering default settings, follow these steps:

1. Use ↑, ↓, →, or ← to position the cursor where the field is to begin.

2. Press F5 to add a field (see fig. 8.8). A list box appears. Column one contains a list of fields in the database; column two displays a list of calculated fields.

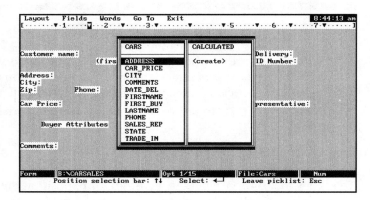

Fig. 8.8
The list box for selecting a field to add.

8

3. Highlight the field to be added.

4. Press ⏎Enter. Structure information about the selected field appears near the top of the screen; the default template appears in the middle of the screen; options and instructions related to modifying the template occupy the balance of the display (see fig. 8.9).

5. Press Ctrl+End to accept the default template. The template XXXXXXXXXX appears above the first name description on the Forms Design work surface.

6. Continue adding fields to the Forms Design work surface. The completed custom form includes character (XXXXX), numeric (9999), date (MM/DD/YY), and logical (L) field templates (see fig. 8.10).

The completed form is ready to be saved and used to view and edit data. Remember that you can press F2 to see the final screen and then return to the Forms Design work surface by pressing ⇧Shift+F2.

184

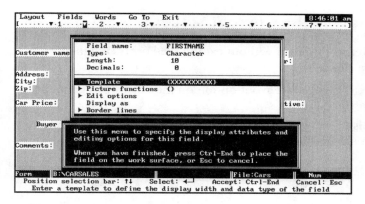

Fig. 8.9
Structure information, the default template, and options and instructions.

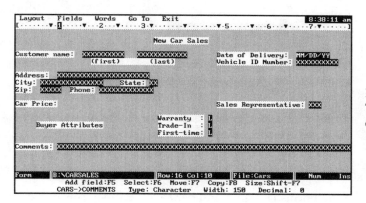

Fig. 8.10
The completed custom form.

8

Saving the Custom Form

You can spend much time creating and testing each custom form. Don't wait until the custom form is completely finished before you store it to disk. Saving your work at regular intervals while you are in the creating process minimizes loss of data in case of a power interruption. Select Save This Form from the Layout menu to store the current form without exiting the Forms Design work surface. You must supply up to an eight-character file name when you save a custom form for the first time.

Also use Save This Form on the Layout pull-down menu to create a new form from an existing form. To do this, select an existing form that is similar to what you want to create. Make the necessary changes and then save the form, giving it a new name.

Exercise 2.3: Saving the Current Screen

To save the current custom screen without exiting the Forms Design work surface, follow these steps:

1. Press Alt + L to access the Layout option on the Forms Design menu bar.

2. Select Save This Form. A prompt appears, requesting a name for the custom screen (see fig. 8.11).

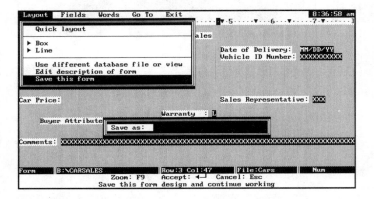

Fig. 8.11
The file name prompt.

3. Enter up to eight characters to specify the file name and press ↵Enter.

Use the Exit option on the Forms Design menu bar to leave the Forms work surface. Select Save Changes and Exit if you are saving the form for the first time or you want to save modifications to a previously saved form. Alternatively, you can choose the option Abandon Changes and Exit.

You can easily fine-tune the layout of a custom screen by using the Move and Copy features described in the next section.

Objective 3: To Modify and Enhance the Layout of a Custom Screen

After you have designed the screen with the field layout and templates, you may need to make changes to the design. Such changes may involve moving and copying fields to new locations. Deleting fields also may be necessary. Remember that this screen should be attractive as well as functional for the user. Therefore, you may need to highlight areas of the screen by using Box and Line draw.

Moving and Copying Fields

You can move or copy any rectangular area of the Forms Design work surface to another position on the work surface. Moving removes the rectangle from one area of the work surface and places it in another location. Copying leaves the rectangle in the original area and duplicates the block in another location. The steps for moving and copying are nearly identical. Both features can include text and fields; however, you cannot move or copy part of a field.

Exercise 3.1: Moving or Copying Part of a Custom Form

To move (or copy) a portion of a custom form, access the Forms Design work surface and follow these steps:

1. Position the cursor at the upper left corner of your choice of rect-angles to be moved (or copied).
2. Press [F6] to mark the upper left corner of the rectangle.
3. Use [↑], [↓], [→], or [←] to highlight the area to be moved (or copied). The rectangle to be moved or copied becomes shaded as you move the cursor.
4. Press [↵Enter] to complete defining the rectangle.
5. Press [F7] to activate Move (or [F8] to copy).
6. Use [↑], [↓], [→], or [←] to move the cursor to the location where the item should be moved (or copied).

   The shaded rectangle appears in its target location.
7. Press [↵Enter] to complete the move (or copy).

8

Removing Fields

When a field is no longer needed on the custom form, remove it by using [Del] or the Fields menu.

Exercise 3.2: Removing a Field from the Custom Form

To remove a field, follow these steps:

1. Position the cursor on the unwanted field template.
2. Press [Del] to remove the template.

The field template is removed; however, the descriptive field name must still be deleted by using [Del] and [←Backspace].

187

You also can use the Remove Field option on the Fields menu to remove all occurrences of a specified field. This method is preferable if the field to be deleted appears in more than one place on the custom screen.

Exercise 3.3: Deleting a Field

To delete a field from a custom screen using a menu option, follow these steps:

1. Press $\boxed{\text{Alt}}$ + $\boxed{\text{F}}$ to access the Fields menu.
2. Press $\boxed{\text{R}}$ to select the Remove Field option.
3. Highlight the field name to be removed. A picklist of field names appears on-screen next to the Fields pull-down menu.
4. Press $\boxed{\text{⏎Enter}}$ to remove all occurrences of the highlighted field.

You have learned to use the basic tools available for creating and modifying a custom screen. One other feature, Box and Line draw, can help you make your custom screens easier to read.

8

Using Box and Line Draw

To enhance custom screens, you can surround groups of fields, text instructions, or even the entire screen with a box. Alternatively, you can separate portions of a screen or a box with a line. Using these two features, you can make your custom screen easier to read, and you can reduce errors by helping users focus on important information. If you choose either the Box or Line option on the Layout pull-down menu, you can choose a single line, a double line, or one of 256 special character symbols.

Exercise 3.4: Using a Box Design

To draw attention to a particular portion of your form, draw a box around the area. The process is similar to highlighting an area to be moved or copied.

Follow these steps from the Forms Design work surface:

1. Press $\boxed{\text{Alt}}$ + $\boxed{\text{L}}$ to access the Layout pull-down menu.
2. Press $\boxed{\text{B}}$ to choose Box. Border styles include a single line, a double line, or a choice of 256 characters from the ASCII character set (see fig. 8.12).

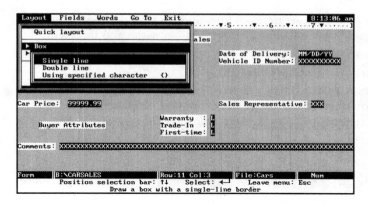

Fig. 8.12
Border styles.

3. Select the type of box border, such as Single Line.

4. Use ↑, ↓, →, or ← to position the box symbol in the upper left corner of the area you want to enclose.

5. Press ↵Enter to anchor the starting point of the box.

6. Use ↑, ↓, →, or ← to draw the lines that form the box.

7. Press ↵Enter to complete the box. The boxed information appears on the Forms Design work surface.

8. Press F2 to view the revised custom screen. The boxed information appears on the custom screen.

9. Press ⇧Shift + F2 to return to the Forms Design work surface. To remove a box, simply position the cursor anywhere on the boxed line. The entire line then changes color. Press Del, and the box will disappear.

To change the shape of a box after it has been placed on the screen, place the cursor anywhere on the box line and press ⇧Shift + F7. The cursor will move to the lower right corner of the box. Use ↑, ↓, →, and ← to change the size of the box. Press ↵Enter to complete resizing the box. (You also could delete the box and redraw it.) Watch the navigation and message lines for guidance in performing these tasks.

Using the Quick Layout Option

As an alternative to specifying each field separately, you can use the Quick Layout option on the Layout menu to transfer at one time all fields to the Forms Design work surface. The resulting display looks similar to the Edit screen because one field appears on each line, and each field appears in the order created. The fields you transfer display the field name and field template; the template reflects the field type and width defined in the database structure.

(Remember that if only selected fields from a database will appear on a custom screen or you want to rearrange the order and placement of many fields, starting the creation process from a blank screen and individually selecting each field is more efficient than using the Quick Layout option.)

Exercise 3.5: Using Quick Layout

To use Quick Layout to transfer all fields in a database to the Forms Design work surface in a few keystrokes, follow these steps:

1. Open the CARS database, highlight Create in the Forms panel of the Control Center, and press ⏎Enter.
2. Press Alt+L to access the Layout menu. The highlight rests on the Quick Layout option.
3. Press Q or ⏎Enter to select the Quick Layout option. The Quick Layout resembles the Edit screen in the Browse mode or Edit mode.

After the Quick Layout custom screen has been created, you can easily make adjustments to the final screen display. Use previously discussed actions to add or remove descriptive text and fields, reposition text and fields, or add lines and boxes.

Objective 4: To Use Templates and Picture Functions

When you design custom forms, you probably expect to use the forms to enter or display data. Whenever you enter or display data in dBASE IV, editing instructions control the data.

Two of the means to control what data can be entered in a field are *templates* and *picture functions*. Templates control individual positions in the data field. Suppose that you create a character field for an inventory part number and you specify a width of 8. Further assume that the first character position always contains a letter, the next two positions always contain a number, the fourth position always contains a letter, and the remaining four positions always contain a number (for example, part number A12X2456). After you add the data field to the custom form, you can customize the template to allow only letters in positions 1 and 4 and only numbers in the other positions.

Picture functions control the entire field. The function symbol ! forces all characters in the field to be uppercase, for example. Templates and picture functions can work at the same time.

Using Templates

When you enter data in Browse mode or Edit mode, each field into which data is to be entered appears in reverse video or a different color. The cursor appears in the first field in which data can be entered. The width of the highlighted data area represents the maximum width of the data field in the database.

When you add a data field to the forms work surface, a highlighted area representing the size of the data field appears at the cursor. On the work surface, the characters you see in the highlighted area form the default template. If you create your own custom form from a blank Forms Design work surface, you see the default templates for each field you place on the form (see fig. 8.13).

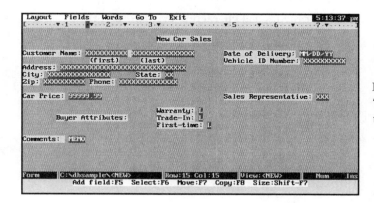

Fig. 8.13
The default templates.

The following table shows examples of how a field data type is displayed in the template.

Field	Template	Code that controls data entry or screen display
Customer Name	XXXXXXXXXXXX	X accepts any character
Car Price	99999.99	9 accepts only a digit or a sign (= or –)
Warranty	L	L accepts only a logical character (Yy, Nn, Tt, Ff)

Templates offer a means to edit data as it is entered in a field. Suppose that you define CITY in a database structure as a character field having a width of 15. If you transfer the CITY field to the Forms Design work surface, you see the default template XXXXXXXXXXXXXXX. Each *X* tells dBASE IV to accept any character in that position.

You can change the template to AAAAAAAAAAAAAAA so that dBASE IV accepts only letters. The template !AAAAAAAAAAAAAA tells dBASE IV to convert the first letter to uppercase (because of the symbol !) and accept only letters in the remainder of the field. Several template symbols are available, as follows:

Symbol	Action
A	Accepts only letters (AENZ, aENz)
L	Accepts only logical characters (Yy, Nn, Tt, Ff)
N	Accepts only a letter or digit
X	Accepts any character
Y	Accepts only logical characters Y or N
9	Accepts only a digit or a sign (+ or EN)
#	Accepts only a digit, a blank, or a sign (+ or EN)
*	Displays leading zeros as *
[blank]	Displays leading zeros as blanks
!	Converts a letter to uppercase
,	Uses commas for large numbers

8

Modifying Templates

Use the Modify Field option on the Fields menu to change a template. Some of your choices include limiting entry to alphabetic characters or forcing alphabetic characters to become uppercase.

Exercise 4.1: Changing a Template

To modify a template, access the Forms Design screen you want to change and follow these steps:

1. Position the cursor on the first character of the template for the field to be modified. Place the cursor on the first character of the First Name field. If the template is properly selected, the field information appears on the message line in the lower portion of the Forms Design screen.

2. Press ⎯Alt⎯+⎯F⎯ to access the Fields pull-down menu.

3. Press ⎯M⎯ to select Modify Field. The upper half of the window contains information from the database structure about the field to be modified. The current template appears in the middle of the Modify Field window.

4. Press ⎯T⎯ to select Template. The cursor appears at the end of the template, and a list of symbols is displayed. Note that an exclamation point (!) converts a character to uppercase.

5. Edit the template to substitute ! for the first character of the first name field.

6. Press ⎯⏎Enter⎯ to accept the new template.

7. Follow the navigation line instructions to press ⎯Ctrl⎯+⎯End⎯ to accept the new settings and restore display of the Forms Design work surface.

The modified template now appears on the Forms Design work surface.

Using Picture Functions

Picture functions control the entry or display of data for the entire field; templates control only individual character positions. You can see templates on the Forms Design work surface; however, you do not see similar codes for picture functions on the Forms Design work surface. The two features can work together to control the entry and view of data, or you can use one or the other. Following are some examples:

8

Case 1: Using both a template and a picture function.

Field: FIRSTNAME

Template: !XXXXXXXXX

Picture function: Alphabetic characters only

Result: When you enter marianne, you see Marianne. When you enter Mar8anne, the computer beeps and refuses to accept the entry. The current picture function doesn't allow entry of a number.

Case 2: Using a picture function only.

Field: SALES_REP

Picture function: Multiple choice (with allowable entries for salespersons with the initials JPT, NAJ, and SDM).

Result: When you move the cursor to the JPT SALES_REP field, you see JPT. Press (Spacebar) and you see NAJ. Press (Spacebar) again and you see SDM.

With the settings described in Case 2, you are not required to type the field contents; instead, press the (Spacebar) until the desired entry appears and then press (↵Enter).

Accessing the Picture Functions Options

The options on the Picture Functions menu vary according to the type of field selected.

Exercise 4.2: Using the Picture Functions Menu

To access the Picture Functions menu, follow these steps:

1. Access the appropriate Forms Design screen.
2. Position the cursor on the field for which you want to establish a picture function, and then press (Alt)+(F) to access the Fields menu.
3. Press (M) to select Modify Field.
4. Press (P) to access the Picture Functions options (see fig. 8.14).

To give you an idea of how the Picture Functions options work, consider two examples using the menu choices applicable to character fields.

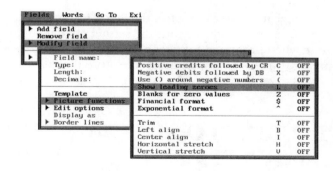

Fig. 8.14
The Picture
Functions options
you see if the field
is numeric.

Using the Scroll in Display Width Option

Suppose that you have in your database a field that is 150 characters long. To
see this field on-screen, you can use the Scroll in Display Width option and
specify a screen display of fewer characters, such as 50 characters. When the
cursor is on this field controlled by a limited display, all 150 characters can be
seen by using → and ← to scroll the contents in the 50-character screen
display.

Exercise 4.3: Using Scroll in Display Width

To choose a picture function option and view the results of using the Scroll in
Display Width option, follow these steps:

1. Position the cursor on the field to be modified.

2. Press Alt + F to access the Fields pull-down menu and then press M
   to select Modify Field.

3. Press P to access the Picture Functions options.

4. Select Scroll in Display Width. You are prompted to enter the scroll
   width.

5. Type the desired width, such as 50, and press ↵Enter.

6. Follow the navigation line instructions to press Ctrl + End enough
   times to restore the Forms Design work surface.

7. Press F2 to display the custom form.

8. Position the cursor on the COMMENTS field template and use → and
   ← to scroll data inside the COMMENTS field of the CARS database,
   which is under the control of a picture function to narrow screen
   display.

9. Press ⇧Shift + F2 to restore the Forms Design work surface.

To modify the scroll width, repeat the steps to select the Scroll in Display Width option and then specify a new width. To turn the setting off, delete the current scroll-width setting when prompted to enter a scroll width, and follow screen instructions to press Ctrl+End enough times to restore the Forms Design work surface.

Objective 5: To Use Edit Options To Control Data Entry

dBASE IV offers nine editing options that give you considerable control over how the user types data. (In earlier versions of dBASE, these editing techniques were available only to programmers.) When adding or editing a field on the work surface, you can associate one or more edit options with the field by using the numeric or character function screens discussed earlier. When the user places the cursor on the field, the edit options begin to work. The options can display on-screen messages to the user, edit data as it is entered into the field, and take appropriate action if the entry is incorrect.

8

Accessing Edit Options

The Edit Options menu enables you to attach as many as nine powerful editing criteria to any field.

Exercise 5.1: Activating the Edit Options

To access the Edit Options menu and access a Help screen to explain the options, follow these steps:

1. On the Forms Design work surface, position the cursor on the field to which you want to attach editing criteria.
2. Press Alt+F to access the Fields pull-down menu and then press M to select Modify Field.
3. Press E to select Edit Options (see fig. 8.15).
4. Press F1 to access Help screens associated with the Edit Options and press Esc to exit the Help feature.

Help screens provide explanations about the options. Also watch the navigation and message lines for additional information.

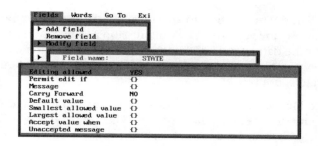

Fig. 8.15
Nine powerful
options appear on
the Edit options
menu.

To accept current edit options, press Ctrl + End until the Forms Design work surface is restored. Press Esc to cancel the current edit option session.

Using Edit Options

If you set the option Editing Allowed to No, a user can view but not change the contents of the field.

Choose the Permit Edit If option to allow the editing of a field only if the stated condition is met. Using the CARS database, for example, you might permit data entry in the COMMENTS field if the WARRANTY field entry indicates no warranty.

Use the Message option to display a message in the lower portion of the screen whenever the cursor is placed on the field. With this feature, you can give a user instructions about how to use the field.

The Carry Forward option causes data from the field in the preceding record to be carried forward to the next record. You can use this feature when you add a batch of records to a database and all the entries for a particular field are the same. Suppose that the contents of a ZIP code field are the same throughout many of the records you are entering. Using this option on the ZIP code field carries forward the ZIP code from the preceding record so that you don't need to retype it. You can edit automatically entered data when you need to.

Use Default Value to place a predetermined entry in the field each time you add a record. If all your records concern customers living in one state, for example, specify the name of the state as the default value. You can edit the value if you need to.

You can establish a smallest allowed value and a largest allowed value to specify a range where the field contents must fall. To limit the entries in a field that contains the month in which dues are due, for example, set the Smallest Allowed Value to **1** and the Largest Allowed Value to **12**. Although this method does not ensure total accuracy, it does prevent gross errors.

You can use the Accept Value When option to specify when the user can type data in the field. You can use any valid dBASE IV expression as the condition. The option does not edit the data; it merely determines when an entry is allowed. You might allow an entry into a vendor name field, for example, only if the vendor number field is not blank.

Through the Unaccepted Message option, you can set up a custom message that displays when the entry to a field is unacceptable. When data being entered in a field is rejected because it does not meet the criteria set in one of the edit options, you want to provide the user with as much information as possible about the problem. If you enter a value of 15 in the DUES_DUE field, for example, the entry is rejected because the value is greater than the largest allowed value. You might create the following unaccepted message:

```
The entry must represent a month between 1 and 12.
```

You can understand how the edit options work by examining two options—Default Value and Unaccepted Message.

Exercise 5.2: Establishing a Default Value and Unaccepted Message

8

To cause the contents of a data field to appear automatically in the field and to specify information to appear in the message line, follow these steps:

1. Access the applicable Forms Design work surface and position the cursor on the field to which you want to attach editing criteria.

2. Press Alt + F to access the Fields pull-down menu, press M to select Modify Field, and then press E to select Edit Options.

3. Select Default Value, and type the contents you want to appear automatically in the field, in this exercise "IN" (see fig. 8.16). Be sure to enclose character data in double quotation marks ("). This value sets up the two-digit code for the state of Indiana as the default value in the STATE field.

4. Press ↵Enter to return to the Edit Options menu.

5. Select Unaccepted Message and then type the information to appear in the message line.

6. Specify additional edit options, if appropriate, and press Ctrl + End until the Forms Design work surface appears.

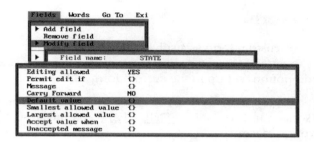

Fig. 8.16
The Default Value
option.

When you add a record, the default value appears automatically in the STATE
field. When you position the cursor on the STATE field, the message you
attached to the field displays in the message line (see fig. 8.17).

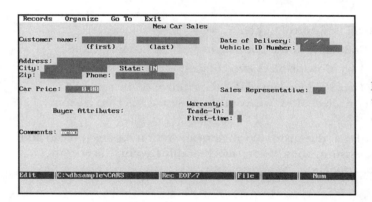

Fig. 8.17
The message is
displayed.

8

Combine any or all of the nine edit options to ensure that the most accurate
information possible is entered in the database.

Objective 6: To Use the Custom Form

All the time you spend creating a custom screen pays off when you see how
your work improves the screen display for data entry or viewing data. You
quickly realize that using the editing features—templates, picture functions,
and edit options—makes data entry pleasant and more accurate. Take the time
to try out your creation, test its built-in editing features thoroughly, and make
changes as necessary. Be sure to store backup copies of your working custom
screens.

Selecting a Custom Form

You can use your completed custom form as a substitute display for Edit mode. Even if you prefer to enter or view data in Browse mode, the templates, picture functions, and edit options set up in the custom form still operate.

Remember that you press [F2] to access the Browse mode or Edit mode from the Forms Design work surface and you press [⇧Shift]+[F2] you return to the original Forms Design work surface.

Exercise 6.1: Selecting a Custom Form

To select a custom form and, in the process, open the associated database, follow these steps:

1. Access the dBASE IV Control Center.
2. Highlight the CARSALES in the Forms panel of the Control Center.
3. Press [↵Enter]. A window displays two choices.
4. Select Display Data to view data under the control of the selected custom screen or select Modify Layout to revise the selected custom screen.

If you select Display Data, the custom form appears in Edit mode; you can add new records or edit existing ones. If you select Modify Layout, the Forms Design work surface appears.

Testing and Modifying a Custom Form

Before you begin extensive data entry using your new custom form, test the form. Enter a number of practice records. Make intentional errors that cause your edit options to work. Try to enter data that is not one of the multiple-choice options available for that field, for example, or try to enter a value that is higher than the maximum value you established for a field. Determine whether your messages say what you want them to say.

Inventory all fields on-screen to make sure that you have not forgotten essential fields. Also check that fields and field names are not reversed. Consider having someone who does not know dBASE test your custom data-entry form. Novice users usually encounter any problems that exist in the operation of a custom screen and often can suggest improvements in on-screen messages.

8

After the testing process or as time passes, your custom form may need to be edited. Perhaps you discover an error in the design or you find erroneous data as you periodically validate your database contents. Decide whether you can make changes to the edit options to prevent errors.

You may need to add or delete fields in your database or change the width of a field. Whenever you change your database structure, be aware that you may have custom forms, reports, or labels to change as well.

Exercise 6.2: Modifying a Custom Form

To change a custom form, follow these steps:

1. Access the dBASE IV Control Center, highlight the form name, and press ⏎Enter.

2. Select Modify Layout to access the work surface and make the necessary changes.

3. Press Alt + E to access the Exit menu from which you can save (or abandon) the custom form you just modified.

Closing a Custom Form

To close a custom form, select a different form from the Forms panel in the Control Center or close the current database file.

Exercise 6.3: Exiting a Custom Screen Display

Follow these steps to exit a custom screen display in Edit mode, close the current database, and close the associated files in other panels:

1. Press Alt + E to access the Exit pull-down menu. Three options appear if you accessed Edit mode from the Forms Design work surface.

2. Select Exit to return to the Control Center.

3. Highlight the name of the open database in the Data panel (an open file appears above the line) and then press ⏎Enter.

8

Chapter Summary

In this chapter you learned to create custom forms to facilitate data entry and improve screen display of data. Many of the features you use to produce a custom form, such as the Editor work surface and the picture functions, also can be used to create custom reports—the topic discussed in the next chapter.

Testing Your Knowledge

True/False Questions

1. The Forms Design work surface is less structured than the Data Design work surface or the Query Design work surface.

2. Each custom form design contains only fields.

3. A field template is a pattern of editing characters that control what type of data can be entered into each character position in the field.

4. Picture functions control the entry or display of data for the entire field.

5. When you change the database structure, custom forms, reports, or labels are changed automatically.

8

Multiple Choice Questions

1. When you create a form without a database or query (view) active, the work surface appears with which pull-down menu displayed?
   A. Fields
   B. Words
   C. Layout
   D. Go To
   E. Exit

2. The template XXXXX, indicates what can appear in the field?
   A. up to five numbers
   B. up to five characters (alphabetic or numeric)
   C. exactly five numbers
   D. exactly five characters (alphabetic or numeric)
   E. up to five X's

3. Moving any rectangular area of the Forms Design work surface to another location

    A. removes the rectangle from one work area and places it in another location.

    B. leaves the rectangle in one work area and places a copy in the new location.

    C. can be done only once.

    D. can be placed only in a location below the original.

    E. removes the rectangle from one work area.

4. Two ways to control what data can be entered into a field are

    A. template and flowchart functions.

    B. skeleton and template functions.

    C. picture and editing functions.

    D. template and picture functions.

    E. template and format functions.

5. All the following are edit options on the Edit Option menu except

    A. Editing Allowed.

    B. Smallest Allowed Value.

    C. Accept Value When.

    D. Accepted Message.

    E. Carry Forward.

Fill-in-the-Blank Questions

1. The template 9999 restricts entry to a maximum of _____ numbers; the template MM/DD/YY accepts only _____.

2. If you choose either the Box or Line option on the Layout pull-down menu, you can choose a _____ line, a _____ line, or a _____ character symbol.

3. Templates control individual positions in the _____ field.

4. If you set Editing Allowed to _____, a user can _____, but not change, the contents of the field.

5. You may need to _____ or _____ fields in your database or _____ the width of a field.

8

203

Review: Short Projects

1. Creating a Custom Screen

   Create a custom screen for the STUDENT database, located in the Class category. Add only the descriptive text and save the form as STUDENT.

2. Modifying the Custom Screen

   Modify the custom screen created in the first short project, and add the field names to the design. Use Move or Copy Fields if needed. Save the form as STUDENT.

3. Adding Records to a Database

   Use the existing form to add three new records to the STUDENT database. Print the screen design.

Review: Long Projects

1. Creating Form Design Screens

   Create a form design screen for the CONTACTS, RESTAURANT, and MUSIC database. Add descriptive fields. Save each form design.

2. Modifying Form Design Screens

   Modify each form design screen for each database used in the first long project and add editing options to each. Test the options and add three new records to each database.

8

Designing Custom Reports

In previous chapters you learned how to list database contents to screen or printer, one record to each line. The report capability is a powerful tool for displaying your data in a variety of formats and with a number of enhancements.

Suppose that you would like to see a variety of items in a multiple-page custom report for a car dealership: the name of the car dealership and the current date at the top of the report; a page number provided on each page; sales data including customer name, car price, and delivery, grouped by salesperson; subtotals of sales made by each salesperson; and a grand total of all car sales. You easily can create such output using the Reports panel in the dBASE IV Control Center.

The report capability can be used in combination with other dBASE IV options. You can select records with a query (such as cars sold by a specific salesperson) and then organize the selected records (by buyer last name, for example) before printing them as a custom report. Other report features include making calculations, counting records, averaging numeric data, and creating other summary information. In a car dealership report, for example, you could create sales commission data as a percentage of car price, and print the average selling price of a car at the end of a report. After you design a report layout that you like, you can save it and reuse that layout as many times as you want.

The dBASE IV Reports panel enables you to create sophisticated custom reports and customized letters. As a manager of data, you benefit much more from custom output than from a mere listing of database contents.

Objectives

1. To Understand the Reports Design Screen
2. To Create a Custom Report
3. To Create Quick Reports
4. To Enhance the Appearance of Reports
5. To Print a Custom Report

Key Terms Used in This Chapter	
Band	An area on the Reports Design work surface related to one of the standard parts of a report. For example, the Page Footer band specifies items that appear at the bottom of every page.
Column Layout	A Quick Layouts option in which field information appears side by side in column format across each printed line of a report.
Form Layout	A Quick Layouts option in which field information appears one field per line.
Mailmerge Layout	A Quick Layouts option for integrating data in calculated fields into a custom form letter.

Objective 1: To Understand the Reports Design Screen

After you study the organization and features of the Reports Design screen, you will find that it makes creating custom reports simple. The screen is organized like all the other Control Center panels. From top to bottom, it includes the menu bar, work surface, status bar, navigation line, and message line (see fig. 9.1).

9

206

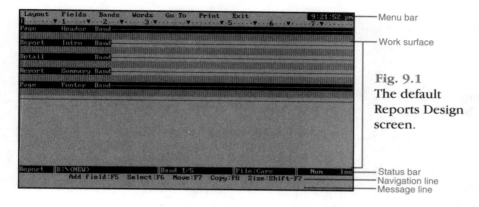

Fig. 9.1
The default
Reports Design
screen.

All but one of the menu bar options appear on other dBASE IV menu bars. The new menu bar option, Bands, is used to enter specifications about the report output format.

Understanding the Work Surface

The Reports Design work surface occupies the area between the menu bar and the status bar. You can attach fields and text to the Reports work surface much like positioning notes on a message board.

Think of each band as a miniature work surface. You explore the use of each band in later sections.

Using the Status Bar

The status bar uses the same general organization and format as other status bars. Some of the information is unique to the Reports Design work surface, however (see fig. 9.2).

When the cursor is on a band border, you see the current band in the status bar; 1/5, for example, indicates the current band (1) out of the total bands in use (5). When the cursor is on a bands work surface, you see the current line and columns cursor position.

207

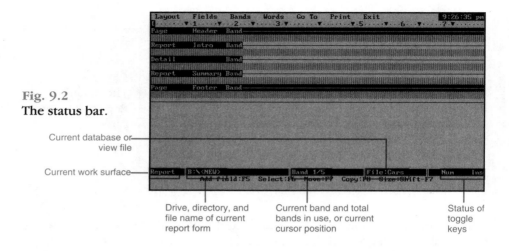

Fig. 9.2
The status bar.

Current database or view file

Current work surface

Drive, directory, and file name of current report form

Current band and total bands in use, or current cursor position

Status of toggle keys

Using the Navigation and Message Lines

Use the navigation line to stay informed about what keys are active at the moment (see fig. 9.3). These keys change while you are copying and moving items on the work surface. Although the key options that appear on the navigation line are the same in both the Reports and Forms work surfaces, the results of pressing those keys are slightly different.

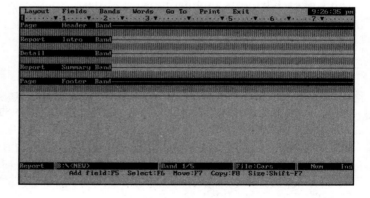

Fig. 9.3
The navigation line.

Press F5 to see a list of fields and then select a field to transfer to the work surface. Press F6 to highlight a rectangle on the work surface. The highlighted rectangle can be deleted, moved, or copied. Press F7 to move the highlighted rectangle to another location on the work surface. Press F8 to copy the highlighted rectangle item. Press ⌨Shift + F7 to increase or decrease the size of a field or box displayed on-screen.

Watch the message line for important instructions and prompts when you are moving, copying, or sizing items on the work surface. You also see instructions about the features you choose from a menu. When you add a field to the reports work surface, for example, each of the Edit options is explained on the message line. Messages also appear if you attempt to use a dBASE IV feature in an incorrect manner.

Planning a Custom Report

Before you begin to work with the Reports Design work surface, you should have in mind a general layout for the custom output. You might set up one report to display data in columns across a page, for example, and set up another report to display data in a custom letter format. You also should plan for enhancements, such as repeating headers and page numbers on multiple-page reports. If you take a few moments to review common report formats and the basic elements of a report, the explanation of bands on the Reports Design work surface will be easy to understand.

Understanding Common Report Formats

Remember that a record in a database is a collection of related fields. Custom reports can include one or more fields from all records in the database or from selected records in the database.

Custom report formats vary in the positioning of the data. dBASE IV generates three common report styles: column, form, and mail merge. Using the column layout, field information appears side by side across each printed line of the report. Each row displays information about one record. Using the form layout, field information appears one field per line. Blank lines separate records. Using the mail merge layout, field information appears interspersed with text in a custom letter. One letter includes information from one record.

If the three standard layouts (called Quick layouts) provided by dBASE IV do not meet your needs, you can create your own custom report formats. After you decide on the general form, you also should determine what items, in addition to data, should appear in the report.

Understanding Basic Report Components

Quite often at least four standard elements appear in a report. These include introductory text, any information repeated at the top of every page, the body of the report, and the summary information at the end of the report (see fig. 9.4).

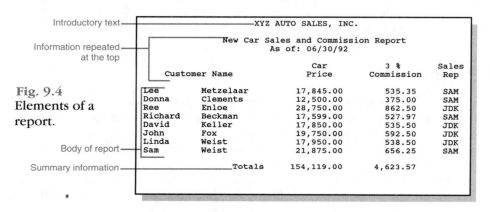

Introductory text

Information repeated at the top

Fig. 9.4
Elements of a report.

Body of report

Summary information

```
                              XYZ AUTO SALES, INC.

                     New Car Sales and Commission Report
                              As of: 06/30/92

                                        Car          3 %        Sales
              Customer Name            Price      Commission     Rep
          Lee      Metzelaar         17,845.00      535.35       SAM
          Donna    Clements          12,500.00      375.00       SAM
          Ree      Enloe             28,750.00      862.50       JDK
          Richard  Beckman           17,599.00      527.97       SAM
          David    Keller            17,850.00      535.50       JDK
          John     Fox               19,750.00      592.50       JDK
          Linda    Weist             17,950.00      538.50       JDK
          Sam      Weist             21,875.00      656.25       SAM

                           Totals   154,119.00     4,623.57
```

Introductory information generally appears at the top of the first page of a report. Other information is repeated at the top of every page in multiple-page output. The body of the report, containing detail information, follows the page heading. Repeating information, such as page numbers, may appear at the bottom of each page. Summary data may appear at the end of a report.

Understanding dBASE IV Report Bands

dBASE IV provides five bands (small work surfaces) on the initial Reports Design work surface on which to specify components of the custom report. These bands are the Page Header band, Report Intro band, Detail band, Report Summary band, and Page Footer band. Each band is related to one of the standard parts of a report and specifies what is printed on the report (see fig. 9.5).

The bands on the Reports Design work surface correspond to the basic elements of a report.

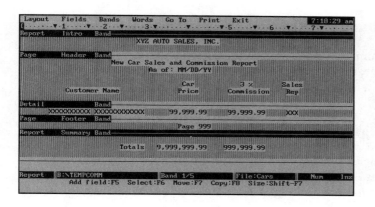

Fig. 9.5
A completed
report design.

Page Header Band

Use the Page Header Band to specify items that are repeated at the top of each page every time you print the report, regardless of how the data changes. In addition to titles and column headings, you might include the current date, a short description of the report's contents, the name of the author of the report, or a page number.

Report Intro Band

A report generally includes introductory text near the top of the first page or on a separate cover page, such as the title and author of the report. Use the Report Intro band to specify this introductory text, which appears only once in the report.

Detail Band

Use the Detail band to set up the body of the report. If you want your data to appear in a specific order, first create a view file using the Query panel and enter sort criteria. If you are creating a sales report using a New Car Sales database, for example, you might sort records by the last name and then by the first name of the buyer. If the report should summarize sales by sales representative, sort the data by sales representative first, and then by customer last name.

9

Report Summary Band

Use the Report Summary band to display grand totals at the end of the report—for example, total car sales in a car sales database. (You also can produce subtotals in a report using optional bands called *group bands*.)

Page Footer Band

A report also can include information repeated at the bottom of every page. You might include a page number, a department name, or the security-related comment *Confidential*. Use the Page Footer band to specify your choice of these repeating items.

As you begin to work with the Reports Design work surface, think about the standard components of a report and the relationship of each to a band on the Reports Design work surface.

Objective 2: To Create a Custom Report

After you have designed your report, you are ready to begin creating the report on the Reports Design work surface. Remember that you can design a report by drawing a new report on paper or by using an existing report produced manually or by other software.

dBASE IV offers two methods for creating a report from the Control Center. You can access a new work surface and construct a report, line by line. dBASE IV also offers a Quick layout feature that you can use if your report conforms to one of three common styles: column, form, or mail merge (the steps to create a report using Quick layout are described in a later section).

Accessing the Reports Design Work Surface

You can work from either a database or view file to create a report. If you use a database file, its fields are all available to be used in your report. If you use a view file, you can choose a limited number of fields to include in your report.

9

Exercise 2.1: Activating the Reports Design Work Surface

To access the Reports Design work surface from the Control Center, follow these steps:

1. Access the Control Center screen, highlight CARS, and then press `↵Enter`.
2. Highlight Create on the Reports panel and press `↵Enter`. The Layout pull-down menu appears when you select Create to access the Reports Design work surface.
3. Press `Esc` to access the work surface.

The Reports Design work surface appears; you can enter report specifications in the bands.

Exercise 2.2: Selecting a Database or View

If you have already accessed the Reports Design work surface and you want to create a report that uses a database or view other than the current one, you follow these steps:

1. Press `Alt`+`L` to access the Layout menu.
2. Select Use Different Database File or View. A picklist window appears at the right side of the screen. Notice that both database (DBF) and view (QBE) file names display in this window.
3. Select the desired database or view.

The Reports Design work surface reappears, and the name of the database or view file you selected appears in the status bar.

To use the Reports Design work surface, enter report specifications in the bands. The cursor marks the current work surface position. If the cursor is positioned in a band, the border of the band is highlighted. As you move the cursor and enter text or fields on the surface of a band, the band gets larger. The display on the design screen duplicates the format of printed output. The shape of the cursor is dependent on the status of `Ins`. When Insert is toggled on, the cursor shape is a large square bullet. If Insert is toggled off, the cursor takes on the familiar shape of an underscore. These attributes are common to all bands.

9

Using the Report Intro Band

When you access a new Reports Design work surface, the bands are arranged in the following order: Page Header band, Report Intro band, Detail band, Report Summary band, and Page Footer band. If you do not want a separate introduction to the report or a separate summary to the report, use the bands in the order given and omit entries in the Report Intro and Report Summary bands.

If you do want a report title that is provided once, but not repeated as part of each page heading, access the Bands pull-down menu and set Page Heading in Report Intro to **No**. When you use the Bands pull-down menu to indicate that page headings are separate from report headings, the order of the bands changes.

Exercise 2.3: Specifying a Nonrepeating Title

To specify a nonrepeating title on the Report Intro band, access the Reports Design work surface and follow these steps:

1. Use ↑ or ↓ to position the cursor in the Report Intro band. The Report Intro band changes color.
2. Press Alt + B to access the Bands pull-down menu.
3. Highlight Page Heading in Report Intro Yes.
4. Press ↵Enter to change the Yes to No.
5. Use ← or → to position the cursor on the Report Intro band work surface and type the appropriate text **XYZ AUTO SALES, INC.** Figure 9.6 shows the centered report title on the first line of the Report Intro band.

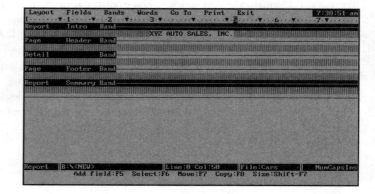

Fig. 9.6
A centered report title.

Using the Page Header Band

Text and data that are to appear at the top and bottom of each page in a multiple-page report should be entered in the Page Header and Page Footer bands, respectively. The contents of these bands are primarily text typed on the work surfaces. If dates, times, record numbers, or page numbers are to be repeated on each page, however, they should be placed on the work surfaces using [F5] (Field).

Pressing [F5] displays a Field window, which includes a column titled Predefined containing the choices Date, Time, Recno, and Pageno. dBASE IV provides the data in these fields. Two fields, Date and Time, get their information from the computer system.

Exercise 2.4: Entering Page Header Specifications

To enter page header specifications, follow these steps:

1. Use [↑] or [↓] to position the cursor on line 1 in the Page Heading band.

2. Use [↑], [↓], [←], or [→] to position the cursor and enter the following:

   New Car Sales and Commission Report

   As of:

   This text information is typed directly into the work surface.

   Rather than typing the date to follow *As of*, you can cause the current system date to display by specifying a Field option.

3. Use [↑], [↓], [←], or [→] to position the cursor, and enter field information. To enter the information, press [F5] to access the fields window, and select each field name to be transferred to the work surface (see fig. 9.7).

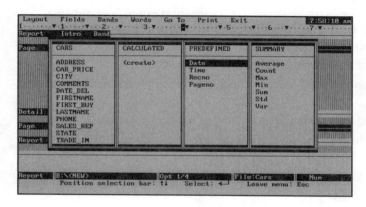

Fig. 9.7
The predefined Date field, highlighted for selection.

4. Press ⏎Enter and then press Ctrl+End to transfer the highlighted field to the work surface. The predefined Date field is transferred to the work surface.

5. Continue to add text and fields to the Page Header band until it is complete.

6. Insert or delete blank lines to establish the desired spacing between the contents of the Page Header band and the band borders.

   Press ⏎Enter to add a line; access the Words pull-down menu, and select Remove Line to remove the line at the current cursor position.

Using the Page Footer Band

Page footers usually contain the page number. Other uses include placing a security statement, such as *Confidential*, on the page or identifying information, such as a report title, department name, or company name.

Exercise 2.5: Entering Page Footer Specifications

To enter page footer specifications, follow these steps:

1. Position the cursor on line 0 of the Page Footer band and then press ⏎Enter to add one blank line to the band. (Entering one blank line at the beginning of the Page Footer band ensures that proper spacing appears between the last Detail line on a page and the page footer information.)

2. Use ↑, ↓, ←, or → to position the cursor and enter text information, **PAGE**. You type text information directly on to the work surface.

   Rather than typing the page number, you can cause automatic page numbering to display by specifying a Field option.

3. Use ↑, ↓, ←, or → to position the cursor, and enter field information (press F5 to access the fields window and select each field name to be transferred to the work surface).

   The predefined Pageno field is highlighted for selection.

4. Press ⏎Enter and Ctrl+End to transfer the highlighted field to the work surface.

   The predefined Pageno field is transferred to the work surface.

5. Continue to add text and fields to the Page Footer band and adjust spacing until it is complete.

Using the Detail Band

The Detail band contains an image of text and data fields that display one record, a detail line, in the body of the report. When the report is printed, the detail line is repeated as many times as required in the body of the page. A detail line will not be divided between pages. If you include a blank line at the beginning or end of the Detail band, then detail lines are double-spaced. A detail line can contain as many lines as necessary to display your data. A Detail band contains mostly data fields and little, if any, text.

Data fields transferred to the Detail band can be one of three types: existing fields in the database, additional predefined fields, and calculated fields.

Entering Character and Numeric Fields

Using the Detail Band, you need to select the fields in the order you wish to print them. When you select the field name, dBASE displays the field type and width as designated in the design structure.

Exercise 2.6: Entering Character Fields

To enter character field specifications into the Detail band, follow these steps:

1. Use ⬆ or ⬇ to position the cursor on line 0 of the Detail band.

2. Use ⬅ or ➡ to position the cursor at the column where the first field is to be transferred to the work surface.

3. Press F5 to access the Fields window and highlight the desired field name. The first name field, FIRSTNAME, is highlighted for transfer to the work surface.

4. Press ⏎Enter to transfer the highlighted field to the Detail band work surface.

5. Specify changes to the Template or Picture function (detailed explanations of templates and Picture functions are provided in Chapter 8), and press Ctrl + End to transfer the field to the work surface.

6. Continue entering character fields, as shown in figure 9.8.

Numeric data is entered on the work surface in the same manner as character data. Most numeric data requires that the edit picture be modified to include punctuation, however. Modifying the edit picture may mean moving the picture on the work surface to ensure alignment under headings.

9

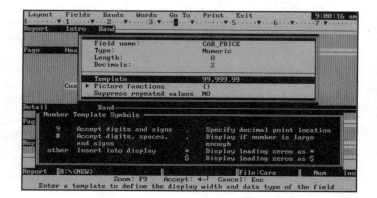

Fig. 9.8
Three character fields (first name, last name, and sales representative) appear on the Detail band.

Exercise 2.7: Entering Numeric Field Specifications

To enter numeric field specifications in the Detail band, follow these steps:

1. Position the cursor in the column where the leftmost character of the numeric field is to appear.

2. Press F5 to access the Fields window and highlight the field name, CAR_PRICE, to be transferred to the work surface.

3. Press ↵Enter to select the highlighted field.

4. Specify changes to the Template or Picture function, as shown in figure 9.9. A comma appears in the printed result if the portion to the left of the decimal point exceeds three digits.

Fig. 9.9
A comma has been added to the template.

5. Press Ctrl + End to transfer the field to the work surface.

218

Entering Calculated Fields

Calculated fields also can be added to the Detail band work surface. To do this, you must first create the field using literal data and an existing field or fields in the database. After the calculated field is created, it can be transferred to the work surface. The Template and Picture function can be edited.

Exercise 2.8: Creating Calculated Fields

To create a calculated field and transfer it to the work surface, follow these steps:

1. Position the cursor in the column where the leftmost character of the calculated field is to appear.

2. Press F5 to access the Fields window, highlight Create in the CALCU-LATED column, and then press ↵Enter. A calculated field window appears on-screen (see fig. 9.10).

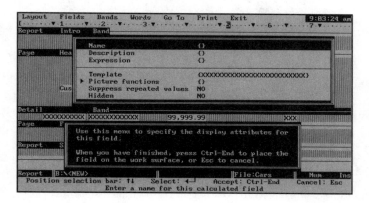

Fig. 9.10
A calculated field window.

9

3. Select Name, enter COMMISSION, the name you want to give the new field, and then press ↵Enter.

4. Optionally, you can select Desc, enter a short description of the field, and then press ↵Enter.

5. Select Expression, enter the expression, CAR_PRICE*.03, that will form the new field, and then press ↵Enter. The formula CAR_PRICE*.03 can be typed or formed, for example, using the ⇧Shift + F1 expression builder (see fig. 9.11).

6. Specify changes to the Template or Picture function.

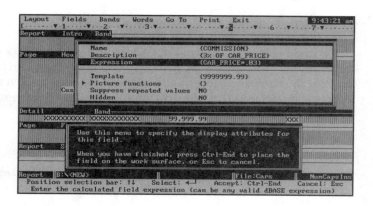

Fig. 9.11
The formula
CAR_PRICE*.03
entered as an
expression.

7. Press Ctrl + End to accept the specifications and transfer the new field to the work surface (see fig. 9.12).

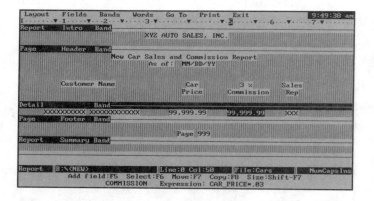

Fig. 9.12
The new field
appears on the
work surface.

When you created calculated fields, two options you did not use were Suppress Repeated Values and Hidden. The Suppress Repeated Values option causes a value in the field to print only once. You may have a field in your database that contains city, for example. Sort the database by city and then set Suppress Repeated Values to Yes. When you print the database, you will have an alphabetic list of all cities. The Hidden option permits you to add fields to the work surface but hide them from view. You may want to add a field (salary, for example) to the work surface so that it can be used in other calculations but not be seen on the report.

To complete the specifications in the Detail band, enter remaining fields, and remove all leading and trailing blank lines from the band to create single spacing in the printed result.

9

Using the Report Summary Band

The Report Summary band is used to specify text and summary data once at the end of the report. The word *Total* may appear on the last line of a report, for example, followed by the totals of numeric data in columns. You have already learned what is necessary to create a Report Summary band: entering text information, adding data fields to the band, and aligning numeric fields on the work surface.

Exercise 2.9: Creating a Report Summary Band

To create a Report Summary band, follow these steps:

1. Use ↑ or ↓ to position the cursor on line 0 of the Report Summary band.

2. Press ↵Enter to add one or more blank lines to separate Report Summary band information from the last Detail band line printed.

3. Use ← or → to position the cursor at the column where the first text is to appear, and type the text, Totals. One blank line separates Report Summary band information from the last detail line. The text *Totals* indicates what information is to appear on the line.

4. Position the cursor in the column where the leftmost character of the numeric field is to appear.

5. Press F5 to access the Fields window, highlight Sum in the SUMMARY column, and then press ↵Enter. A summary field window appears on-screen. Create a summary field the same way you create a calculated field.

6. Select Name, enter the name TOTAL, and press ↵Enter.

7. Optionally, you can select Desc, enter a short description of the field, and then press ↵Enter. The summary field description indicates a computation on the CAR_PRICE field.

8. Select Field to summarize on, enter the numeric field name to be summarized, CAR_PRICES, and then press ↵Enter. Car prices are then totaled and the sum displayed.

9. Specify changes to the Template or Picture function.

10. Press Ctrl + End to accept the specifications and transfer the new field to the work surface. The new summary field appears on the work surface.

11. Continue entering fields in the Report Summary band. Figure 9.13 shows a completed Reports Design work surface.

9

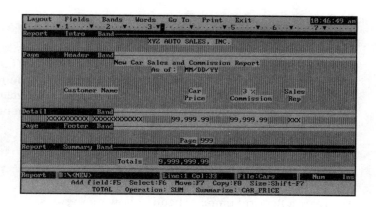

Fig. 9.13
The completed
Reports Design
work surface.

The work surface is complete and ready for a trial printing. Before printing, however, save the work surface.

Saving the Report Design

The importance of saving the report design cannot be emphasized enough. Always save the report when it is completed. Even while you are developing the work surface, you should save your work and continue editing. Power failure, keyboard lockup, and many other interruptions could destroy all your hard work.

Exercise 2.10: Saving the Report Design

To save your work and continue editing the work surface, follow these steps:

1. Press [Alt] + [L] to access the Layout pull-down menu.
2. Select Save This Report, CARS.
3. Respond to the prompt for a file name. Specify the path and file name used to save the current specifications on the Reports Design work surface.

If this procedure has been used earlier, you will see a file name in the Save As box. If it is the correct file name, simply press [←Enter] to save the file. If the name is not correct, delete the box contents and then enter the correct file name.

Exercise 2.11: Saving and Exiting the Reports Design Work Surface

To save the specifications on the Reports Design work surface and exit to the Control Center, follow these steps:

1. Press Alt + E to access the Exit pull-down menu.
2. Select Save Changes and Exit.
3. If prompted for a file name, enter the name.

If you entered the work surface using the Create option in the Reports panel, you will be prompted for a file name when you save the report specifications. If you are modifying an existing report, however, it is automatically saved under its original name.

Objective 3: To Create Quick Reports

The Quick Layouts option on the Layout menu helps you build a report design with little effort. Two of the quick layout choices, Column and Form, copy all fields in the database or view to the Reports Design work surface. The fields appear in the order they were created in the database or described in a view. You then can modify the standard quick layout if necessary by adding text, changing the description of field names, and rearranging fields. A third Quick Layouts option, Mailmerge, lets you create a standard form letter and then merge specific data from records (such as name and address) to automate the preparation of mass mailings.

Before you use the Quick layout options, you may want to create a query that controls the output. In the view skeleton, you can specify your choice of fields—and the order of those fields—to appear in the custom report. This action can eliminate unnecessary fields and control field order when fields are automatically transferred to the work surface in a Quick Report layout. In the file skeleton, you can establish selection criteria to limit records to those meeting stated conditions and sort criteria to print those records in a specified order.

Using the Column Layout

If you choose Column Layout from the Quick Layouts menu, fields appear side by side in column format across the printed line. The current date and a page

9

number are automatically placed in the Page Header band along with the field names, which are used as column headings. All data fields not restricted by a query are distributed across the Detail band. Total fields for numeric or float data fields appear in the Report Summary band.

If you simply want to produce a column layout report of the current database or view, and you don't want to modify the standard report, press ⎄Shift + F9 (Quick Report) in any Control Center panel. You can rearrange the data fields, add text, or add heading and group subtotals, however, by choosing Column Layout from the Quick Layouts menu in the Reports panel.

Exercise 3.1: Accessing the Quick Layout

To access the Quick Layouts option and create a column layout for a custom report, follow these steps:

1. From the Control Center, open the desired database, CARS.
2. Highlight Create on the Reports panel and then press ⏎Enter.
3. Select Quick Layouts. Three layout options appear (see fig. 9.14).

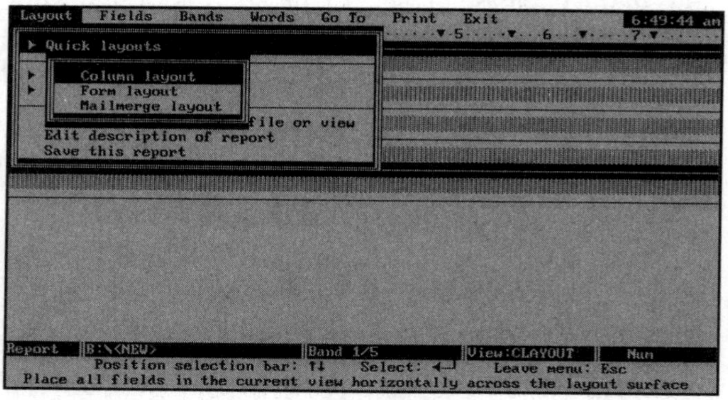

9

Fig. 9.14
Three layout
options.

4. Select Column Layout.

Field names from the current file appear automatically in the Page Header band arranged in columns across the page.

Fields from the file appear automatically in the Detail band arranged in columns across the page.

You can customize the report by adding a report title. If you place the title in the Page Header band, the title repeats on each page of the report. If you place the title on the Report Intro band, the title appears once on the report's first page.

To modify the initial column layout, follow the same procedures used to change a custom screen (details are provided in Chapter 8). To delete text or fields in a band, for example, use F6 (select) to highlight the area for deletion and press Del. To rearrange the items on the Reports Design work surface, highlight the area needing change and press F7 (Move) or F8 (Copy).

When the report is complete, save it to disk using the option Save Changes and Exit from the Exit menu on the Reports menu bar or the Save This Report option on the Layout menu. To print the report from the work surface, choose the option Begin Printing on the Print menu bar.

If you exit and save the report design, you also can print the report from the Control Center. Highlight the name of the report on the Reports panel, and press ⏎Enter. A window appears displaying three options: Print Report, Modify Layout, and Display data. Choose Print Report.

Using the Form Layout

If you choose Form Layout from the Quick Layouts menu, fields appear one field per line, just as they do in Edit mode. The page number, fields, and column titles appear in the Page Header band. To create, customize, save, and print the new report, follow the same procedures used with Column Layout.

9

Using the Mailmerge Layout

The Mailmerge Layout option is one of dBASE IV's major new features. If you choose Mailmerge Layout from the Quick Layouts menu, you access a form on which you can create a standard letter that integrates data fields from the database into the body of the letter.

After you choose the Mailmerge quick layout option, you see a blank report form. No text or fields have been added to this layout screen. All bands except one are closed; the Detail band is open and in word-wrap mode. Because word-wrap mode functions like a word processor, you can create your custom letter on the Detail band.

Suppose that you want to send a personal letter to each customer listed in a new car sales database. The letter might congratulate the customer on a recent purchase of a new car and include an offer for a free oil change.

The standard letter you create with Mailmerge Layout is the same for each recipient. You can add several fields of data from each person's record, however, to personalize each letter. Using the Mailmerge Layout option, you can enter the field names for first name, last name, street address, city, state, and ZIP code, and then dBASE pulls the specific names and addresses for each letter from the database. Use the following example as a guide for developing your own custom letters.

Exercise 3.2: Accessing Mailmerge

To access the Mailmerge work surface and create a custom letter, follow these steps and see figure 9.16 for the appropriate text:

1. From the Control Center, open the desired database, CARS.

2. Highlight Create on the Reports panel, press ⏎Enter, and select Quick Layouts.

3. Select Mailmerge Layout. The initial Mailmerge layout screen appears; the Detail band is open and in word-wrap mode (see fig. 9.15).

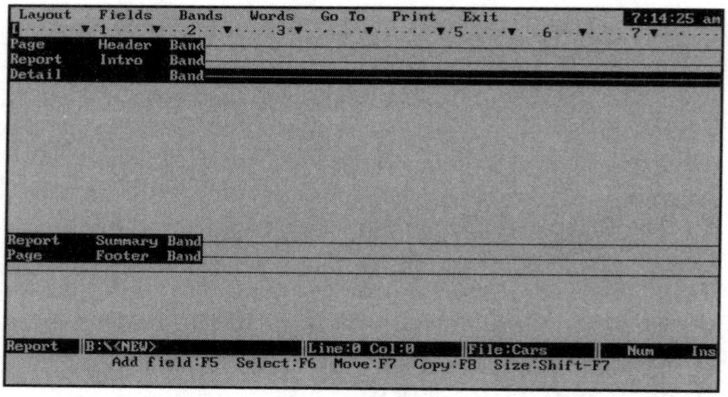

9

Fig. 9.15
The Mailmerge
layout screen.

4. Type the company heading (or press ⏎Enter to insert blank lines if you use letterhead paper) and add a date.

5. Press F5 repeatedly and select fields for the customer's name and address.

6. Move the cursor to the greeting line, type the word **Dear**, add the appropriate name field (such as customer first name), and finish the greeting with a comma.

7. Type the body and closing lines, including fields where appropriate (such as the date a customer bought a car), in order to personalize the letter (see fig. 9.16).

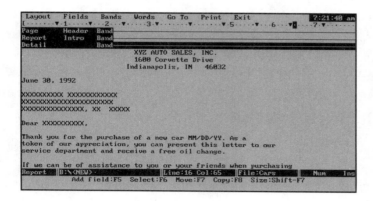

Fig. 9.16
Mixing text and fields in a Mailmerge layout.

Periodically save the Mailmerge report by using the Layout menu option Save This Report. To preview the custom letters, follow the procedures to print from the work surface. When the Print menu appears, choose View Report on Screen. Continue viewing your custom letters, making necessary changes to the report until you are satisfied with the design.

Objective 4: To Enhance the Appearance of Reports

You have learned to create a custom report and to use a query file to select and organize your records before printing. You can print the reports without further adjustments. You may want to enhance the printing you have specified, however. dBASE IV provides several options to enhance the printed report, including selecting the print size and quality of print. You also can emphasize portions of the report using bold, underlining, and italic print styles.

Selecting Text Style

dBASE IV supports six type style settings—Normal (the default), Bold, Underline, Italic, Raised (Superscript), and Lowered (Subscript)—that dress up your

227

printed reports and focus the reader's attention on specific information. Enhanced printing is dependent on the printer you are using. You should consult your printer manual about these features. Most printers however, can produce these basic enhancements.

Text in any band on the report can be styled by accessing the Words menu on the Reports Design work surface. Use F6 (Select) to mark the area on the label that is to be enhanced. After the area is selected, use the Style option on the Words pull-down menu to choose the enhancement.

Exercise 4.1: Italicizing a Field

To italicize a field on a report, access the Reports Design work surface and follow these steps:

1. Position the cursor in the upper left corner of the area to be enhanced.
2. Press F6, and use ↑, ↓, ←, or → to highlight the field to be enhanced (see fig. 9.17).

9

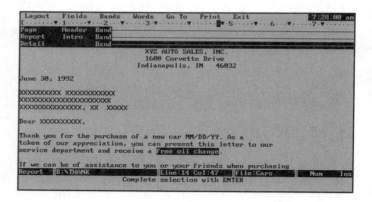

Fig. 9.17
The phrase *free oil change* is highlighted at the end of the first paragraph.

3. Press Alt+W to access the Words pull-down menu and choose Style. The Style menu displays six common enhancements. A list, numbered 1 through 5, contains user fonts (typefaces) also used to enhance text. The five options are blank if you have not installed the custom fonts.
4. Highlight the desired enhancement, such as Bold, and press ↵Enter to turn the feature ON.
5. Press Alt+P to access the Print pull-down menu, and then choose Begin Printing to print the report.

You can see the enhancements only when you print the report. Text style enhancements do not appear on the Reports Design work surface or the screen that displays when you choose the View report on screen option.

Selecting Text Pitch and Quality

Additional options to enhance your printed report involve print size and quality. You normally select a print size for its readability. Nonproportional type sizes are usually described in terms of *pitch*, referring to the number of characters per inch (cpi) that can be printed. On most printers, a 10-pitch type is the default, which means that 10 characters per inch are printed. Often you must choose a smaller print size, however, so that you can display more characters on a line. Your options of print size are pica (10 cpi), elite (12 cpi), or condensed (16 to 17.5 cpi).

Print quality can be specified as default, draft (print quality off), or letter quality (print quality on). You must make two primary considerations in setting print quality on. First, if you have a laser printer, you see little or no difference in the quality of print. When using a dot-matrix printer, however, you notice a considerable difference in quality of output and print speed. In print quality mode, characters are printed twice and appear to be fully formed. The printer speed is reduced significantly, however. You may want to do all test printing with print quality off and then turn on print quality for final production printing.

Text pitch and quality are usually specified for the entire report by choosing appropriate options through the Control of Printer menu accessed through the Print pull-down menu. If you want to apply these settings, such as condensed print for a footer, to a band in the report use the Bands pull-down menu.

Exercise 4.2: Activating Text Pitch and Quality

To choose these two options from the Bands pull-down menu on the Reports Design work surface, follow these steps:

1. Access the Reports Design work surface for an existing report file (or create a new report file).
2. Position the cursor in the band for which you want to alter text pitch and quality.

9

3. Press [Alt]+[B] to access the Bands pull-down menu and highlight Text Pitch for Band.

4. Press [↵Enter] (or [◆Backspace]) until the desired text pitch appears on-screen (see fig. 9.18).

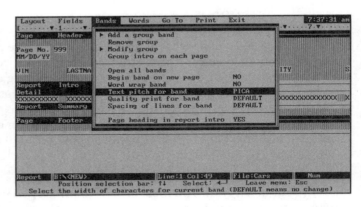

Fig. 9.18
Selecting a pica text size for the current band.

5. Highlight Quality Print for Band.

6. Press [↵Enter] (or [◆Backspace]) until the desired quality setting (Default, Yes, or No) appears on-screen (see fig. 9.19).

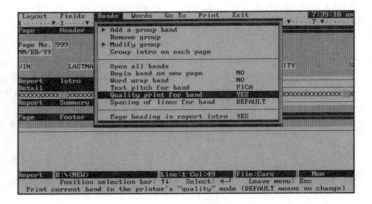

Fig. 9.19
Setting quality print on for the band.

7. Press [Esc] to exit the Bands options.

You can print at this point by choosing the Begin Printing option from the Print pull-down menu on the Reports Design work surface. If you save the report design for repeated use in the future, you will do most of your printing from the Control Center.

Objective 5: To Print a Custom Report

After a report file has been created, tested, and saved, it is normally printed from the Control Center screen. If a query is to control report output, put the appropriate query in use before you highlight the report file name and press `⏎Enter`.

Exercise 5.1: Printing a Report

Follow these steps to invoke a query and print a report from the Control Center:

1. Highlight any query name in the Queries panel of the Control Center relating to the CARS database and then press `⏎Enter`.
2. Highlight the desired report name, CARS, in the Reports panel of the Control Center and then press `⏎Enter`.
3. Select Print report.

Chapter Summary

In this chapter you learned to create custom reports. You have now learned about many of the features of dBASE IV to create and manipulate database files, as well as to produce well-formatted reports for management decisions.

9

Testing Your Knowledge

True/False Questions

1. The Reports Design work surface occupies the area between the menu bar and the status bar.
2. Use the Report Intro band to display grand totals at the end of the report.
3. The Detail band contains an image of text and data fields that display one record in the body of the report.
4. The Report Summary band is used to specify the text and summary data once at the end of the report.
5. Text in any band on the report can be styled by accessing the Fields menu on the Reports Design work surface.

Multiple Choice Questions

1. The default Reports Design screen includes a(n)
   - A. menu bar.
   - B. work surface.
   - C. error line.
   - D. record number.
   - E. both A and B.

2. dBASE IV automatically generates three common style reports:
   - A. column, rows, and form.
   - B. column, form, and mail merge.
   - C. rows, form, and mail merge.
   - D. form, mail merge, and envelope.
   - E. letterhead, mail merge, and form.

3. To set up the body of the report, use the
   - A. Report Summary band.
   - B. Report Intro band.
   - C. Page Footer band.
   - D. Detail band.
   - E. Page Header band.

4. Data fields transferred to the Detail band may be one of three types:
   - A. existing fields in the database.
   - B. formatted fields.
   - C. suppressed fields.
   - D. calculated fields.
   - E. both A and D.

5. Text in any band on the report can be styled by accessing which option on the reports design work surface?
   - A. Layout menu
   - B. Fields menu
   - C. Words menu
   - D. Print menu
   - E. Go To menu

Fill-in-the-Blank Questions

1. Using the _____ layout, field information appears one field per line.

2. Use the _____ band to display grand totals at the end of the report.

3. Numeric data is entered on the work surface in the same manner as _____ data.

4. If you _____ and _____ the report design, you can also _____ the report from the Control Center.

5. You can emphasize portions of the report using _____, _____, and _____ print styles.

Review: Short Projects

1. Creating a Column Report

   Create a column report using the STUDENT database located in the Class category.

2. Creating a Quick Report

   Create a Quick report using the PRODUCTS database located in the Inventory catalog.

3. Creating a Mailmerge Layout

   Create a Mailmerge layout using Quick report. Use the CONTACTS database in the Business catalog.

Review: Long Projects

9

1. Create a Column Report Using All Bands

   Create a column report and enhance the report using the RESTAU-RANT database. Be sure to use all the bands.

2. Creating a Mailmerge Layout Using Quick Report

   Use the CONTACTS database, and create a Mailmerge layout using Quick report. Send an announcement of an opera performance to all contacts that have OPERA as a common field. Be sure to enhance the report appropriately.

Index

G-I